GRAPHIC DESIGN
RANTS
AND
RAVES

GRAPHIC DESIGN

RANTS

AND

RAVES

BON MOTS ON PERSUASION, ENTERTAINMENT, EDUCATION, CULTURE, AND PRACTICE

STEVEN HELLER

Allworth Press books may be purchased in bulk at special discounts for sales promotion, corporate gifts, fund-raising, or educational purposes. Special editions can also be created to specifications. For details, contact the Special Sales Department, Allworth Press, 307 West 36th Street, 11th Floor, New York, NY 10018 or info@skyhorsepublishing.com.

20 19 18 17 16   5 4 3 2 1

Published by Allworth Press, an imprint of Skyhorse Publishing, Inc.
307 West 36th Street, 11th Floor, New York, NY 10018

Allworth Press® is a registered trademark of Skyhorse Publishing, Inc.®, a Delaware corporation.

www.allworth.com

Cover and interior design by The Collected Works

Library of Congress Cataloging-in-Publication Data is available on file.

Print ISBN: 978-1-62153-536-2
Ebook ISBN: 978-1-62153-539-3

Printed in China

THREE

GRAPHIC DESIGN AS VISUAL DIALECT

FOUR

GRAPHIC DESIGN AS CULTURAL MEMORY

ACKNOWLEDGMENTS

I have to rave about Tad Crawford, founder and publisher of Allworth Press, whose advocacy of design publishing earns him a place in any pantheon. A large percentage of all books devoted to design writing have come from Allworth with Tad's enthusiastic leadership. Thank you, Tad.

A book is not a book without editors. Thanks to Zoe Wright and Kelsie Besaw, my editors on this project. And a book is made concrete through its design. Thanks to Justin Colt and Jose Fresenda of The Collected Works, for their splendid design and art direction.

This particular collection culls essays from various print and online outlets where I am a contributor. Gratitude to *Print* magazine's Zachary Petit, who edits my print and Daily Heller copy; the *Atlantic* online's Spencer Kornhaber and Sophie Gilbert; *Wired*'s Robert Gonzales; *Design Observer*'s Jessica Helfand, Eugenia Bell, and Betsy Vardell; *Eye* magazine's John Walters.

For continuous support, I am indebted to David Rhodes, president of the School of Visual Arts (SVANYC).

Many colleagues have also contributed in so many ways. Lita Talarico, Esther Ro Schofield, Ron Callahan, Mirko Ilic, the late Dr. James Fraser, Jim Heimann, Seymour Chwast, Greg D'Onofrio, and Patricia Belen; Veronique Vienne, Gary Taxali.

Finally, I would be nowhere without the love of my wife, Louise Fili, and son, Nick Heller.

Thanks so much.

INTRODUCTION

BON WHATS?

With the ripeness of old age, one has a modicum of maturity with a dollop of wisdom. As a consequence, recently my rants have become less frequent (and, as it turns out, so have my raves). I am experiencing a blossoming of tolerance and now appreciate design ideas that used to annoy me—like geometrically rigid Modern design, which is now among my favorite formal methods.

Being a longtime "critical fan" of graphic design has fueled my work as a researcher and chronicler of the field—a field I chose to join when I realized that, with my drawing skills that were one step above those elephants that paint landscapes, I'd never be a successful illustrator. I fell passionately in love with publication design, type and image, and art direction. Still, I had to do these things on my own terms, which involved refusing to attend any design school or take remedial classes of any kind. In fact, I never received an undergraduate degree in anything, though I do have two Fine Arts honorary doctorates.

As the self-described rebel, I eschewed design annuals and magazines so as not to be overly influenced by others and, shortsightedly, retain a sense of blank-slate purity. I set up straw dogs that I rebelled against (including a few legendary designers who became my best friends). However, I couldn't help but see some designers' work, including that of Frank Zachary, George Lois, and Mike Salisbury, who I selected as my models. Funnily, I had to acquire appreciation for the work of Paul Rand, Seymour Chwast, and Alvin Lustig, all of whom I have since written much about.

Ultimately, writing replaced designing and art directing, and for the past thirty years, I have surveyed, assessed, commented on, and reported on graphic design history and contemporary practice so that a growing number of design students, practitioners, and even an increasing lay audience would learn about our unique design legacy. With that goal in mind, I not only wrote conventional showcase profiles and case studies for design magazines, I ventured into contextualizing graphic design within a social, political, technological, and cultural milieu for the likes of the *New York Times*, *Atlantic*, and *Wired* online. This evolved into deeper critiques.

Back in the 1970s and 1980s, there was a gentleman's agreement not to portray work in negatives. To be featured in one of the leading trade magazines—*Print, Art Direction, Communication Arts, Graphis,* among them—is an honor. Back-patting was de rigueur, and few designers really and truly wanted critical journalism that would tackle graphic design in the same manner common to books, film, theater, and architecture. Although there were academic journals, notably *Visible Language*, that drilled deeply into design as a cultural phenomena and theoretical pursuit, the trade journals were less likely to stray from professional reportage. However, the tenor of the discourse changed in the late 1980s.

As though particles in the Hadron Collider, technology and pedagogy collided, fused, and exploded, the fallout was a kind of reprise of the 1920s and 1930s when aesthetic and philosophical rifts divided traditional or classical from avant-garde modern designers. A lot was happening in hot house design schools. In certain cases, dogmatic rants developed into solid criticism. In the late 1980s, the premiere of England's *Eye* magazine, founded by Rick Poynor, opened a platform for critics that had not existed. I was energized writing for *Eye*. *Print*, where I did most of my survey, profile, and historical writing, gave me space in "The Cold Eye" column for any criticism I wanted to write. It was a double-edged sword of sorts: I learned that many thin-skinned designers only favored design criticism when it was not about their work (as with humor, the definition of comedy is when someone other than you falls on a banana peel). A few acquaintances turned a cold shoulder to me owing to opinions I wrote.

Critiquing friends' work is always tricky. But when I write about design phenomena I am on less-precarious turf. I can rant and rave without fear of making enemies or insulting friends. I realize this is not how a true critic should behave—personal favor should not enter into the process. However, I know too many of the designers I respect and a few of those I do not. What's more, I prefer to write stories about the impact of designed things and design on things.

The terms "rants" and "raves" suggest that the essays in this book are more subjective and personal than objective history and reportage. That is partly true. I would call some of these essays critical commentaries and others historical critiques. I address issues as well as objects, always attempting to provide context and tell an enlightening story. As the subtitle says, these are bon mots (although the jury is out on the bon) on design and design-related things that are researched and reported with elements of theory, commentary, and speculation.

I'm not even clear sometimes which is rant or rave. I'll let you, the reader, decide. But each story has relevance to me and virtue to the field. Whether ranting or raving, as a man of few bon mots, I enjoyed writing them.

01

GRAPHIC DESIGN IS POWER

GRAPHIC DESIGN IS POWER

—

GRAPHIC DESIGN CAN BE MEASURED BY HOW EFFICIENTLY IT MAKES AN IDEA CONCRETE. AS AN AGENT OF POWER, GRAPHIC DESIGN SUPPORTS A MESSAGE AND THE MESSENGER WITH THE GOAL OF INFLUENCING, INSPIRING, AND COMMANDING ATTENTION THAT RESULTS IN ACTION. TYPE AND IMAGE DO NOT WIELD THEIR OWN POWER, BUT WHEN FUSED TOGETHER, THE POSTER, BOOK COVER, ADVERTISEMENT, MAGAZINE COVER, OR USER EXPERIENCE MUST TRANSCEND CLICHÉ AND STARTLE OUR SENSES. SOME GRAPHIC DESIGNS ENTER THE SUBCONSCIOUS; SOME HAMMER THE POINTS HOME. POWER OCCURS WHEN THE RESULT MAKES US STOP, THINK, AND DO.

TYPE AS AGENT OF POWER

WHEN TYPOGRAPHY IS USED TO TEACH, CAUTION, AND COMMAND.

"Teeth are an agent of power in man," wrote Elias Canetti in , his brilliant discourse on the pathology of "packs" and crowds.

"Teeth are emphatically visual in their lineal order," explained Marshall McLuhan in the essay titled "The Written Word" in . "Letters are not only like teeth visually," he continued, "but their power to put teeth into the business of empire building is manifest in our Western history."

What you are about to read is not, as the above might imply, peppered with periodontal metaphors. Rather, the premise of this essay is that letters, when formed into certain typeface styles and families, are agents of power and tools of the powerful. Some are used to gnaw away at freedom of thought and deed, expressing authoritarian dictates. Conversely, certain faces represent those who fight power. Often, these are one and the same face.

So chew on this: typefaces are the incisors of language. In fact, typography, asserts McLuhan, "created a medium in which it was possible to speak out loud and bold to the world itself. . . . Boldness of type created boldness of expression."

In this sense all type wields power. Yet the majority of typefaces in the world are neutral; they communicate ideas from all quarters—left, right, and center—sometimes all at once. Typography is, after all, a "crystal goblet," void of intrinsic ideology. Nonetheless, some typefaces have become putative logos of dogma and doctrine. Germanic black letter (fraktur), celebrated during the Third Reich for its virtues, was the Nazis' "ideal German typeface" and will be forever tainted as a reminder of Hitler's crimes against humanity. Anyone who has seen the spiky black letter masthead of the viciously anti-Semitic Nazi weekly will experience the magnitude of the typeface's evil representation.

Typefaces that exude power spell out commands, convey orders, and announce decrees, which ultimately govern human behavior. The choice of types to serve this purpose is not just an aesthetic decision, but a deliberate means to force people to or or or and Typefaces that demand compliance succeed, in large part, because they are invested with symbolic attributes culminating in real consequences.

Of course, are the real messages and typefaces are only messengers (remember what "they" say about not killing the messenger). Yet the marriage of type and word (and image too) determines tone, tenor, and weight of expression. Visualize the common stop sign. In addition to its iconic octagonal shape bathed in red, the bold sans serif S-T-O-P—notably set in the rigid ClearviewHwy typeface—invariably trips a cognitive switch that compels obedience to such an extent that any sign set in the same demonstrative lettering style has equivalent power. Substitute other "action" words for stop and the initial impact is the same.

Shepard Fairey's famous Obey the Giant logo (like a George Orwell Big Brother Is Watching You poster) is a case in point. Obey is a kind of stop-sign word, made even more imposing through bold, gothic typography. The viewer may not be entirely certain who or what to obey, but following orders is the act that the typeface effectively coerces. Likewise, the words cwhen set in black san serifs, are just as psychologically, not to mention linguistically, powerful as

But could these words have the same impact on the average psyche if they were set in Bodoni, Garamond, or Clarendon? Can types designed for power even have serifs? Heavy slab serifs notwithstanding, do fine line serifs slow down reading and provide the receiver with a millisecond of contemplation time, which could mean the difference between acquiescence and disobedience? Power, you might say, is in the lack of details.

Japanese propaganda magazine, 1941-45, Russian-influenced graphic design by Hiromu Hara.

"The phonetic alphabet is a unique technology." McLuhan wrote in . "Only alphabetic cultures have ever mastered connected lineal sequences as pervasive forms of psychic and social organization. The breaking up of every kind of experience into uniform units in order to produce faster action and change of form (applied knowledge) has been the secret of Western power over man and nature alike." And as the phonetic alphabet developed during the typographic age, the power to control human actions increased in exponential ways. "That is the reason why our Western industrial programs have quite involuntarily been so militant," McLuhan adds with certainty, "and our military programs have been so industrial. Both are shaped by the alphabet in their technique of transformation and

Fraktur lettering (Volk Lettern) from Nazi-era instructional manual, c.1936.

control by making all situations uniform and continuous. This procedure, manifest even in the Greco-Roman phase, became more intense with the uniformity and repeatability of the Gutenberg development."

Only when universal literacy was embraced during the nineteenth century did typography become a tool of authority and typeset words, multiplied through mass printing, did its bidding. This, in turn, triggered chains of events that changed the world. "Of the many unforeseen consequences of typography," McLuhan wrote, "the emergence of nationalism is, perhaps, the most familiar. Political unification of populations by means of vernacular and language groupings was unthinkable before printing turned each vernacular into an extensive mass medium."

Governmental, ecclesiastic, and institutional typefaces— designed at the behest of the state, church, or industry—are not necessarily faces that exert the most overt or oppressive power. Indeed showing brute strength is not always the desired goal of these entities. Types that wield power are stolid and brutish; they scream rather than whisper their messages. Ambiguity is VERBOTEN! It is a safe bet that most nationalist propaganda that attempts to alter minds relies on big, bold typography, which embodies the big, bold nation or state. Consider the variants of the famous World War I recruitment poster, which in the United States reads "I Want You!" For each iteration—German, American, Russian, and so on—the poster's voice derives from a "screamer" headline. Screamer is the term used to describe tabloid newspaper headlines (EXTRA, EXTRA!) and even carnival posters (STEP RIGHT UP!!). Types of power are not solely the tools of those in power. They are perfect simply for selling things—any things. But they can also easily serve the needs of those who wish to be empowered.

When German artist and graphic commentator Käthe Kollwitz, whose son Peter was killed in one of the first battles of World War I, created the 1924 poster "Nie Wieder Krieg" (War Never Again!) depicting a young man holding up his defiant arm over which the lettering is scrawled with litho crayon, she made the most striking of all postwar cautionary emblems. Although this was not a typeface per se, it nonetheless possessed attributes of power. Her emotional scrawl commanded that the human race end its savagery. In the same way, the anarchist magazines (1928) and (1947) employ hand-scrawled and -brushed lettering as mastheads to evoke the power of the masses. It contrasts with the famous Hitler election poster from 1932, where the only typography is a sans serif HITLER (with a square dot over the I) under a stark portrait of the "big brother." The stark, geometric typeface possesses an architectonic authority that suggests, ironically, a forceful yet modern persona.

Obey (Obey the Giant)
Sticker art by Shepard
Fairey, 1989–today.

Numerous typefaces and hand lettering abound with the power to turn statements from rhetoric into action. During World War II a preponderance of sans serifs were used to convey authority. The Italian Fascists, for example, veered from classical Roman letterforms toward stylized "fascist modern." On one hand there existed customized "futurist" typefaces that symbolically suggested speed and progress; on the other were the bold sans serif capitals, a new approach to ancient Italian epigraphy. Type in Fascist Italy was used to approximate the voice of the dictator Benito Mussolini. Since sloganeering was a strategic principle of Il Duce's internal state propaganda to sway Italians toward fascist thinking, the most effective lettering was an essential consideration. Mussolini spread his oratorical power through modernistic gothics that transmitted his proclamations. Yet as emblematic as his faces of power were, they were easily co-opted by his enemies—the Communists, for instance, employed some of the same typographic tropes in their own propaganda. Silly as it may sound, when fighting power with power, stealing or co-opting an iconic typeface can undermine the opponent's powers. When successful, proprietary typefaces are as endemic to visual identity as are trademarks and just as easy to undermine.

Power is a construct that transcends mere typeface analysis. Type is only as powerful as the force behind the message. But power is cumulative and a critical mass of many components of which type and typography are involved. Bold visceral statements and pronouncements are among the bulwarks of power and the apparatus of dissent.

USA typographic specimen showing bold and shadow type from the Klingspor Foundry, Germany, 1920s.

Gioventu Fascista (Young Fascist magazine) Handlettered Futurist-style lettering, 1929.

FDR DEAD
Screamer or
"wood" headline
for NY *Daily
Mirror*, April
13,1945.

FASCIST SEDUCTION

BENITO MUSSOLINI'S EUR WAS ART AND ARCHITECTURE REPRESENTING MODERNITY AND LONGEVITY OF TOTALITARIAN ROME.

There was a bright side to Benito Mussolini's iron-fisted Italian Fascist regime. Even Winston Churchill asserted in 1927 that if he were an Italian he would have given Mussolini his "whole-hearted" support "from start to finish." Mussolini made the trains run on time—and they still do more or less. But more important, as the supreme overseer of Italian culture, DUCE was responsible for creating striking graphic design and startling architecture (including many railway stations). The most notable "relic" of his regime is Esposizione Universale Roma, known as EUR, the white marble and limestone city-within-a-city in the southwestern part of Rome, originally designed to be the new Fascist capital. Some critics say EUR is a blend of classical and rational into a brutish kind of modernist kitsch, but on a recent visit there I experienced a curiously seductive beauty like that exuded by ruins of ancient imperial palaces. It arguably transcends its past ideology. EUR is anything but a ruin. Today it is a functioning residential, governmental, and cultural district. Nonetheless, enemies of totalitarian dictatorships—and I count myself as one—argue that such architecture will always be tainted. Maybe, but I believe one can be fervently anti-fascist and still admire—indeed savor—aesthetics for their own merits.

However, just writing this, I am haunted by a passage from George Orwell's *1984*, in which Big Brother chillingly asserts, "The ideal set up by the Party was something huge, terrible, and glittering—a world of steel and concrete, of monstrous machines and terrifying weapons—a nation of warriors and fanatics, marching forward in perfect unity, all thinking the same thoughts and shouting the same slogans, perpetually working, fighting, triumphing, persecuting—three hundred million people all with the same face."

EUR was designed to tout that notion. And while dystopic art and design should not be celebrated, understanding the underlying motives for design is not celebration. Even being fetishistic about artifacts born of dubious movements and ideologies is acceptable when the overarching context is understood.

Inscriptions in the Roman style were common on the EUR buildings. This was taken from a speech of Benito Mussolini:"A nation of poets, of artists, of heroes, of saints, of thinkers, of scientists, of navigators, of migrants."

Signature of Fortunato Depero made as a mosaic.

EUR, also known as E42, is a vivid example of how something designed to signify one charged entity (the dominance of the Fascist party over the individual) can be transformed into another benign one (a residential and working environment), if only by circumstance (losing the war). Or stated another way, just because the Fascists conceived, designed, and partially built it (it was only completed after the war), that doesn't mean over time it cannot be neutralized—or even redeemed. Yet, to be honest, I realize that the plan, buildings, and sculptures are imposing in a manner that only an adulation-addicted dictator with a Caesar complex could conjure. Therein lies the paradox. Knowing the motivation yet still "appreciating" the outcome suggests deeper psychological complexity rooted in how effectively stirring or soothing is the power and impact of propaganda—EUR was propaganda-architecture.

EUR was scheduled to open in 1942, initially as the ANNO XX commemorative exposition. In the long term, it was intended to expand the city limits of Rome; but more consequentially, it was to be the symbolic capital of Mussolini's new empire (shades of Nelson Rockefeller's Capital Mall in Albany, New York). Designed to echo the grandeur of the Roman Forum, it also was meant to situate the Fascist corporate state in a progressive spotlight. Fascist propaganda hinged on the ability of the party's exhibition designers to engage public passions. They were brilliant. The Anno X anniversary exhibition, for instance, designed by the Futurist Enrico Prampolini, was a masterpiece of scale (large totems and typographic panels juxtaposed with the minutiae of power). DUCE wed art and design to architecture and public spectacle to present his manufactured narrative, and it worked—at least, in terms of his cult of personality. Whatever the motivation and long-term results, some unique design, notably typography and environmental display, existed under Fascist rule.

Fortunato Depero's mosaic mural,
1937–38, celebrating art and science in fascist state.

Mussolini's embrace of Italian Futurism (albeit briefly) suggested a more progressive outlook than the aesthetically reactionary German Fuhrer, Herr Hitler; DUCE's architectural preferences were certainly less gothic and medieval. While Mussolini extolled the style and trappings of ancient Rome (i.e. the Roman salute and the fasci emblem), he allowed for cross currents of Classicism and Modernism to run through Fascism, which contributed a bit of Mediterranean flair. To this day, the remnants of Fascist style continue to be subtly evident in Rome. Having just spent a week there with students as part of a design workshop, I watched how seduced some where by the Fascist facades and block letter inscriptions. Indeed, some drew inspiration for making original typefaces through their own interpretation of classic and fascistic lettering.

What surprised me, however, was how totally taken I was by EUR's centerpiece, Palazza della Civilita Italiana, with its precisely Roman-lettered inscription atop all four sides of the structure, a six story white box evenly punctuated by eight arched openings across and six down (presumably symbolizing the name Benito [down] Mussolini [across]). It is the image in so many di Chirico paintings of fascist town squares. While EUR is imposing both in its volume and mass, it is also curiously more manageable than Hitler's nonbuilt superannuated Germania in terms of the height and breadth of the structures. The Palazzo, which is also known as the Colosseo Quadrato, or Square Colosseum, because its arches echo the landmark Colosseum, is the tallest structure of the complex and sits impressively alone on a small hill, is unencumbered by other structures, is starkly graphic against the sky, and is surrounded by a base of white limestone stairs, grass, and heroic marble sculptures. From a distance, on the way to the airport, it is the most impressive structure on the horizon.

The Palazza is complimented by a number of other fascist buildings, including the Museum of Roman Civilization, with its impressive colonnades resembling centurions standing at rigid attention. Although the uninformed visitor might never know all these structures (most of them constructed on the original plan after the war, in the early fifties) had any negative ideological connotations, one cannot help but feel a certain weight of oppressive architectural power. What's more, unlike Germany, where every trace of the Nazi era has been destroyed, the signs of fascism (in the spirit of preservation) have not been entirely erased, and the epigraphic

Palazzo della Civiltà Italiana, also known as the Colosseo Quadrato (Square Colosseum), is the centerpiece of EUR.

columns, friezes, and manhole covers, as well as a pair of stunning mosaics by Fortunato Depero and Enrico Prampolini that are full of signs and symbols, remain.

EUR is not the Roman Forum (in fact, today it is a very high-rent district), but walking through is like being in Mussolini's head. As a leader of a nation where architecture and design has signified so much, his goal to create an environment that would inspire and overwhelm, rouse and dwarf, was up there with other leaders who envisioned the city as their personal monument of immortality. Of course, anyone who lives amid New York City's powerful architecture may be blasé to this, but not this New Yorker. I admit I was in awe.

The modern EUR Santi Pietro e Paolo a Via Ostiense.

Photos by Mauro Zennaro.

An entrance guarded by imperial eagles at the Museo della Civiltà Romana.

WHEN BOOK JACKETS MEANT FREEDOM

WEIMAR GERMANY MARKED A PERIOD OF POLITICAL AND CULTURAL TURMOIL WHEN BOOK COVERS AND JACKETS OF THE PERIOD FOUGHT OPPRESSION.

The fourteen years of Weimar Germany were a period of politics and cultural turmoil. World War I had decimated the male population and bankrupted the nation. From the ashes of the defeated Empire arose Germany's first democracy and its mortal reactionary enemies. None-theless, censorship was briefly curtailed, and as book collector Jürgen Holstein recently told me, "liberals and above all left-wingers saw the possibility of gaining a hearing for their ideas. New groups were constantly cropping up with new ideas." And this is the focus of *The Book Cover in the Weimar Republic* (Taschen) (originally it was a limited edition titled *Blickfang*) wherein he refers to Weimar as "Postwar—the War after the War," due to the intensity of the debates.

Through the lens of German book publishing from 1919 through 1933 and over one thousand covers, jackets, and bindings, Holstein addresses in eighty profusely illustrated chapters the "hot topics," which are eerily similar to today's issues, including equality for men and women, abortion, and safeguards for youth, as well as an outpouring of books on art and artists, flying and traveling, America and Russia, sports and health, children's books, and much more. The most original of the era's book designs came from publishing houses with left-wing or liberal leanings. "Their founders were usually young," Holstein explains, "and their excursions into the world of publishing often lasted just a few years, after which they disappeared for ideo-logical, but above all for financial reasons (inflation and the world economic crisis)." It is no coincidence that these publishers took chances with cover art since "when it came to design, conservative publishers were seen as homely and old-fashioned."

There was also a practical commercial reason for the flood of novel German book designs. To use their presses to capacity, newspaper publishers like Ullstein, Mosse, and Scherl expanded their publishing programs to include illustrated journals and magazines and also founded book-publishing divisions that competed with the existing book publishers. Consequently, commercial artists were put to work designing jackets and covers in prodigious quantities—and without the oversight of marketing departments as in today's competitive environment.

The artists and designers included many to emerge from several influential graphic art institutions directed by famous commercial artists (Paul Renner, Jan Tschichold, F. H. Ehmcke, E. R. Weiss, Emil Orlik, G. A. Mathéy, etc.) and were located in Berlin, Leipzig, and Munich. The apparent copying of certain approaches was encouraged. Although Holstein notes that there was no canonic style, as there had been around 1900 with Jugendstil (art nouveau), a modern spirit prevailed. "Everything was being tried out then, and it is exciting to see what was possible in just a few years: New Objectivity, Expressionism, Naturalism and Abstraction, the extensive use of photography and collage (unlike in most other countries), and a striking amount of left-wing political literature with a 'modern' design."

Das Lustige Buch cover by Franz Peffer.

These modernists were only loosely associated and for the most part independent artists who became freelance designers as a way to avoid going hungry in those difficult times. And that is the reason for the surprising appearance of Max Beckmann, Hans Bellmer, Max Pechstein, George Grosz, Rudolf Schlichter, El Lissitzky, and the like. Among the most famous and important book designers and illustrators often associated with specific publishers in the Weimar Republic were Herbert Bayer, Georg Salter, John Heartfield, Jan Tschichold, George Grosz, Hans Meid, Fritz Helmuth Ehmcke, Emil Rudolf Weiß, and others. Of these, quite a few eventually emigrated to England and the United States, where they continued to design jackets.

Jack der Auschliher

This book is based on the extraordinary collection built over about ten years, although it was not originally planned as a definitive "collection." "Instead, my wife and I, as regular visitors (and exhibitors) at numerous book fairs, bought books that appealed to and interested us for very different reasons," Holstein explained. Today the collection is held by the Zentral- und Landesbibliothek Berlin.

The wide range of approaches is exciting for various reasons. This is the first accessible critical mass of fiction, nonfiction, art, textbooks, and children's book covers and jackets ever assembled. And although German design magazines covering this fourteen year period often featured surveys with tip-in originals of jackets, there has never been a thematic historical resource to address the context, contents, and creators of the books through expert voices of publishing and design scholars. What's more, it is sobering that the work presented in *The Book Cover in the Weimar Republic* so clearly influenced design between the wars up to and including today.

100% cover by John Heartfield.

Bordell cover by Cesar Klein.

Kunstschaffen un Kunsterleben cover by Will Faber.

Deutschland so Oder so?

Glühende Welt

CAN POSTERS STILL CHANGE THE WORLD

ONCE THEY HELD SWAY BUT CAN THEY STILL MOTIVATE, INSPIRE, AND CALL FOR ACTION AGAINST THE LATEST MASS MEDIA?

In 1987, commuters in New York City started seeing posters on the street reading "Silence = Death." The images were the work of the pioneering AIDS-awareness group ACT UP, and their stark simplicity made an immediate impact.

Two years later, the organization had a graphic-design arm, Gran Fury, which produced a new poster that appeared on the sides of buses showing three couples kissing, two of which were same-sex. Their message: "Kissing Doesn't Kill: Greed and Indifference Do." As works of both art and activism, the ACT UP posters gave a face to same-sex couples, inspiring compassion and encouraging awareness of what the group described as "government inaction and public indifference" to the AIDS crisis.

Such was the power of public images to transmit targeted messages long before the advent of social media. From Ben Shahn's anti-H-Bomb design to the Guerrilla Girls' campaign against gender inequality in art museums, posters have a long history of engaging and informing people through a mixture of artistry, wit, and economy. It would be easy to assume that posters have lost some of their impact in a hyperconnected landscape. But in many ways, the rise of social media has given protest and advocacy posters a bigger audience than ever before, while platforms like Facebook are creating ways to let users craft images featuring their own photos to further the causes they identify with.

This doesn't mean posters aren't facing challenges in the Internet age. Commercial ads and billboards are almost always placed in approved venues, and have adapted well to the new technology of the twenty-first century, with many featuring QR codes, video sequences, and even facial-recognition software. But the humble advocacy poster is printed with ink on paper and usually hung illegally on buildings, lampposts, and hoardings replete with the "post no bills" imperative. Since most of those locations are controlled by commercial businesses that guard their real estate, they're often removed before they can be seen by more than a handful of people.

"No one cares about posters anymore, except the designers who make them," says the graphic designer Matteo Bologna. Posters, he implies, are often simply feel-good portfolio pieces that do more for their designers' careers than for the cause they're seeking to raise awareness for.

But a number of images, placed by guerrilla campaigners in a large number of spots late at night, have gotten themselves noticed. In 2014, posters designed by the street artist Banksy appeared as if by magic on Capitol Hill, featuring an image of a small girl wearing a headscarf and letting go of a red balloon. Below the image was the message #WithSyria—encouraging viewers to explore the hashtag to understand the poster's message, and replicate it by posting the image online themselves.

Banksy isn't alone in his belief that the medium is still alive. "Posters are a practical way for passionate artists to communicate important ideas and play a role in shaping that public sentiment," says Aaron Perry-Zucker. "You don't choose a channel or type in a URL to see them. They come to you as you walk down the street."

Perry-Zucker is the cofounder of the Creative Action Network, an online community of artists and designers who help raise awareness and funds for various causes. CAN bridges the gap between digital and analog by using crowd-sourcing methods to acquire and distribute printed posters from contributors. In addition to campaigns advocating for such diverse issues as gun control, funding for libraries, and marriage equality, CAN recently launched a collaboration with Earthjustice, a group of environmental lawyers, for a campaign called "JoinThePack," to increase understanding of the plight of the endangered gray wolf. Posters and shirts are sold for twenty-five to thirty dollars.

End Bad Breath.

End Bad Breath, 1967. Seymour Chwast skewers the Vietnam War.

"The strength and beauty of a well-designed poster cannot be beat," says Mark Randall, the cofounder of Design Ignites Change, a New York–based firm that has engaged in grassroots social-advocacy campaigns for more than a decade. "A poster lodges in your memory more than other mediums because it distills an idea to its core. [It] becomes a brand statement around the issue it represents."

Randall is currently collaborating with the group Make Art with Purpose (MAP) to develop a nationwide public-art initiative empowering teams of community representatives, artists, and designers to create posters, public murals, and banners that address themes connected to race and social justice. "The images are not a means to an end," says Randall. "The goal is to support and continue the public dialogue around one of the most pressing issues of our time."

Randall agrees that contemporary posters must be part of an overall media strategy and

Plakat und Plagiat, 1915. Special edition of *Das Plakat* on plagiarism.

"should move people to do something tangible." Yet he notes that some posters become iconic on their own owing to a confluence of events and timing. These include Milton Glaser's 2001 design *I Love NY More Than Ever,* Shepard Fairey's 2008 Hope poster, and the meme-ified British World War II sign imploring viewers to "Keep Calm and Carry On."

Social media also allows new viability and greater distribution for posters through the countless sharing opportunities on Facebook, Tumblr, Instagram, and personal websites. "Before digital technology, you had to be out of your home environment. Now, anyone with access to the Internet can view them," says Elizabeth Resnick, a curator of the Massachusetts College of Art exhibition *The Graphic Imperative: International Posters for Peace, Social Justice and the Environment* 1965–2005. "The world of the poster is now available to anyone on a very personal basis. How we interact with posters has completely changed, and because of their accessibility, people have altered the way they view and respond to them."

L'Affiche, April 1927. A review of art, printing, and advertising.

Earlier this year, following the Supreme Court's landmark ruling on same-sex marriage, Facebook allowed users to cover their profile pictures with a rainbow filter, making their images posters expressing solidarity with the movement for marriage equality. In some ways, the rainbow posters were the perfect twenty-first-century heir to the AIDS awareness posters designed by Gran Fury, adding millions of faces to the gay-marriage movement, on a platform more visible and widely accessible than earlier designers could have dreamed of. Posters, Resnick says, are made for causes, issues, and campaigns that need "a kick of emotion and energy—issues that are widely understood, but need more action."

Posters by Peter Bankov from 2013–15: "I draw posters on the plane, in airports and taxis, and during the lectures and business meetings with clients."

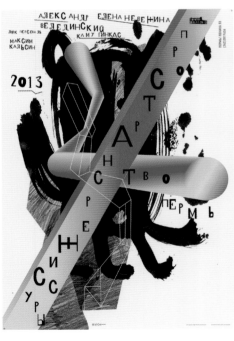

ON THE FRONT LINES OF FREE EXPRESSION

THE MASSACRE OF TWELVE EDITORS AND CARTOONISTS AT THE OFFICES OF CHARLIE HEBDO WAS NOT AN ISOLATED EVENT.

In 1968 the arts, culture, and satire magazine *Evergreen Review* featured the story "The Spirit of Che" with a now-famous deific portrait of Che Guevera by Paul Davis on both the cover and posters throughout the New York City subway. This iconic illustration was so offensive to anti-Castro Cubans that they bombed the Evergreen offices in Greenwich Village. Fortunately, no one was hurt.

Well, that's not exactly true. Free expression took a hit.

Anyone with the fanatical need to access mass media could apparently do so through violence. In 2016 the media is more accessible than ever to anyone with an Internet account, yet it is so densely populated that the magnitude of violence has risen exponentially to be heard and seen above the din.

The massacre of twelve editors and cartoonists at the offices of *Charlie Hebdo*, the French satiric weekly that prides itself on humorous attacks of any and all folly, is not an isolated event, albeit the bar has been raised. As this was a premeditated killing spree over a newspaper's satiric content, it could be seen as a new license for others. But satire, satirists, and cartoonists have long been targets.

In France the satiric press has a history of being squelched through legal and extra-legal means. Honoré Daumier, France's greatest cartoonist, who in 1832 published an offensive, antigovernment cartoon, *Gargantua,* was jailed for six months. "Between 1815 and 1880 about twenty French caricature journals were suppressed by the government and virtually every prominent nineteenth-century French political caricaturist either had his drawings forbidden, was prosecuted and/or was jailed," writes censorship scholar Robert Justin Goldstein. In 1918, in the United States, contributors to *The Masses* were brought to trial charged with "unlawfully and willfully . . . obstruct[ing] the recruiting and enlistment of the United States," owing to a Henri Glintenkamp cartoon showing a skeleton measuring a man for a coffin with the title *Physically Fit.* During the early twenties, cartoonist/caricaturist George Grosz endured three criminal trials for "public offense" owing to his caustic attack on the German military in his portfolio *Gott mit uns.* Had Grosz stayed in Nazi Germany, where there was a warrant for his arrest, his cartoons would have put him in a concentration camp.

Graphic commentators are often on the front lines of the war for free expression. And today they are even more vulnerable to religion-mandated assassination. Free expression continues to take a hit. The cartoonist and editor of *Charlie Hebdo,* Stéphane Charbonnier, who was killed yesterday, had said, "We have the right to express ourselves, they have the right to express themselves, too."

However, murder is not expression.

Charlie Hebdo cover, January 14, 2015, a week after two Islamist attackers killed twelve staffers. The sign uses the phrase "Je Suis Charlie." The headline reads: "All is forgiven." *Courtesy Veronique Vienne.*

PEEPING IN

PRINT MAGAZINE EXPOSES HOW SEX AND DESIGN'S LONG-TERM RELATIONSHIP HAS BEEN SULTRY AND TUMULTUOUS.

The pillow talk between sex and graphic design has been going on almost as long as commercial art has existed—well over 150 years. Strange bedfellows? Not really. Sex is practiced and sexuality is shown in virtually every conceivable art form dating back to the Egyptians' more risqué hieroglyphics. So this is no sordid affair. Sex is endemic to the very definition of graphic design.

Type and type casting are imbued with sexual innuendo—including the impression or "kiss" of a type slug of metal on paper—ooh la la. There are also promiscuous relations between a matrix (mom), produced by a punch (dad) that gives birth to the typeface (kid), which are all part of a family. There's even something called a hickey, when a speck of dust adheres to the printing plate and creates an imperfect outcome. (Makes you wonder, what came first? The term for this printing flaw or the adolescent's make-out blemish-of-honor?

Graphic design's sexuality is ofttimes veiled in nuance—left to the eye of the beholder, as it were—but aspects of it are far from pure and innocent. If we widen the peephole to see how graphic design has been intertwined with sexuality, we'll find that it ranges from implied to explicit.

The theme of this issue of *Print* is sex and graphic design, but I believe our focus should be more precisely on sex in graphic design—and even more definitively on sex in advertising. Sex in design is a communication tool that provides eye-grabbing solutions to certain content demands and design problems. Sex is bait that lures the viewer into the message. What sex isn't is a typeface or other formal design element alone. There are plenty of sexy images produced by hard-core illustrators, photographers, and designers each year, but graphic design is actually neuter, neither male nor female, a clean slate. A designer can inject sex appeal into design through word and picture, but unlike a piece of clothing, for instance, a piece of graphic design is never inherently sexy.

What is sexy in this context, anyway? Let's be honest, until recently what we called "sex" was primarily the depiction of women in wanton and alluring poses, wearing sensual garments or nothing at all, strategically employed to capture the audience's attention. In fact, and it's no surprise, the recurrent and widespread exploitation of women has long been a major feature of advertising, marketing, and publishing (ads, packages, and book and magazine covers), with hints of eroticism and a bit of masochist menace at its core.

The depiction of sexuality in design media has nonetheless radically changed after decades of pushing boundaries: Once the most risqué image a publication or advertisement could show was a woman's bare ankle. As designers slowly worked their way up the leg, thighs and hips became acceptable; then other titillating parts of the human body were exposed for all to see. Not too long ago, nudity of any kind was prohibited from American print, TV, and films (Europeans had much fewer Puritan hang-ups). Then, one by one, antiquated prohibitions vanished overnight. First came cheesecake, the quaint term used to describe artsy frontal nudity. From there, mores changed quickly, yet simply: First backside nudity was revealed, then frontal nudity, and ultimately, genitals were exposed in both males and females. There was even a time when women modeling bras were prohibited from being shown on TV, forcing adolescent young men to scour the *New York Times Magazine* for its generous selection of print ads. Eventually, public opinion (at least the opinions of people I talk to) accepted that which was once considered pornography as daily media fare.

Try this new definition on for size: sex is now anything that surrounds, supplements, complements, leads up to and/or finalizes a sexual act—whatever the various imaginative options may be. Even mass advertising (witness those sex-enhancing drug ads and contraceptive commercials) has taken prurience by the horns, pandering to society's fixation with sex.

Still, it's worth repeating that graphic design is no more inherently sexual than it is overtly political or religious. To be even clearer, graphic design is an objective frame in which a range of tropes, from sexual suggestion to outright hard-core pornography, is presented. There is, for instance, no typeface or typography that's sexy enough to trigger lust or desire—not even the oft-tried trope where naked people are arranged to make individual letters. Yet when type is set into words, and layouts are filled with soft-core, erotic, or even lewd drawings or photographs, graphic design enhances the sexuality by telegraphing meaning and message. In this case, sex is in the eye of the maker. Only when the intent of a designer is to inject sex into an ad, for example, does graphic design actually become sexual.

But who can deny there has been, and still is, a surfeit of sex in graphic design. Some eras have enjoyed more sexual license than others. This is arguably a libertarian age for overt sex in media. Yet during the "Victorian" 1950s, when television husbands and wives were required to sleep in separate beds, sex could only be implied, if at all.

Sex in graphic design has obviously evolved, but from what? Was there an original sin, a moment when some printer, layout person, or art editor combined apples and oranges and created nasty mojo? If so, it's not chronicled. Over the past 150 years, roughly the span of what we now call graphic design, there have certainly been various questionable images sent off as trial balloons, testing the mores of the day. Some have been banned as unbefitting or distasteful to proper society. However, censorship doesn't only occur in matters of overt or implied sex; most times the censor's scissor cuts words for political or religious blasphemy and words with sexual messages can be too hot to handle.

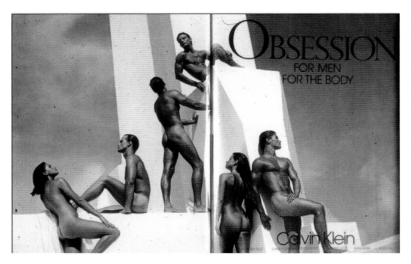

Here's a personal example: In 1968, I was the "art director" for an underground sex tabloid called *Screw*. The original masthead or logo, which I did not do, was amateurishly scrawled and plain ugly. Although a novice myself, I wanted to change it, so I selected a typeface from the

Various examples of how sex, sexuality, and sensuality have been used in popular culture from advertisements for fragrance and cigarettes to liquor and books.

Photo Lettering Inc. catalog and ordered SCREW in big bold, slab serif letters. A day later, when I arrived to retrieve the proof, I was told they wouldn't typeset obscenity (even though the typesetters all read the magazine). I later learned the decision-makers were afraid of being arrested simply for setting a word that ended up in a pornographic publication. This is probably the only time that a type house refused to set five letters citing pornography as a reason. "We've come a long way, baby!" to paraphrase the 1968 Virginia Slims advertising campaign that exploited women's liberation to sell cigarettes specifically to female consumers (sex objects by any other name). There are still a few virgin areas of art and design that remain untouched by sexual tropes; however, graphic design, advertising, and industrial and product design are driven more by sexual concepts, metaphors, and symbols than ever before. Chastity isn't always a virtue. The following vintage examples reveal how sex has been used not simply to titillate through overly literal methods but as nuanced gestures, too. Let the peep show begin.

WANTED

THE RISK-TAKING MAGAZINES OF RALPH GINZBURG HAVE THE POWER TO DRIVE THE ESTABLISHMENT MAD.

It was not difficult for Ralph Ginzburg to look like an arrested pornographer in the 1968 advertisement titled "Wanted." He was, after all, convicted of violating a federal obscenity law by using the mail to promote *Eros*, the hardcover magazine that celebrated love and eroticism, and he would eventually serve eight months in a federal facility as punishment for his crime. By his own admission, he published the most controversial, taboo-busting magazines of the twentieth century and, by my estimation, authored some of the most provocative text-driven promotional ads of any century. He was a brazenly committed pitchman for his landmark publications, two of which, *Eros* and *Fact*, were driven out of business by the legal system.

Meanwhile, the newer, no less risqué *Avant Garde* was gathering its circulation. Ginzburg mastered the grit and bravado of direct advertising. His full- and double-page advertisements like "Wanted," weighing in at over four thousand words, were used similarly to the way crowdsourcing is used today: to generate interest and harvest subscription dollars, often in advance of publication. "Wanted" is decidedly one of his most compelling ad concepts.

When "Wanted" first ran in *Evergreen Review* in 1968, Ginzburg was awaiting a Supreme Court decision on his appeal for the 1963 obscenity conviction (the appeal was denied in 1972 and led to the prison sentence). The ad, which his lawyers would have preferred he forgo so as not to antagonize the court, was a hard-sell manifesto-cum-promotion that explained the *succés de scandale* of *Eros* (declared obscene by the USPS), *Fact,* which questioned presidential nominee Senator Barry Goldwater's psychological fitness, and *Avant Garde*, which Ginzburg called "a pyrotechnic, futuristic bimonthly of intellectual pleasure."

Readers of the periodicals where Ginzburg's ads appeared were predisposed to reading text-heavy stories, so why not text-heavy advertisements too. It was a gamble that paid off. The ad prose was spritely and often written in the third person. "Wanted" started as a paean to Ginzburg's accomplishments: "Pictured above is Ralph Ginzburg, publisher of the most notorious

WANTED

Pictured above is Ralph Ginzburg, publisher of the most notorious and wanted magazines of the 20th Century.

First he launched the quarterly **Eros**, a magazine dedicated to the joys of love and sex. **Eros** was an instantaneous *succès de scandale* and over a quarter of a million people ordered subscriptions, despite the fact that they cost $25. But the U.S. Post Office declared **Eros** "obscene" and drove it out of business (and, incidentally, obtained for Ginzburg a five-year prison sentence, which has since been appealed).

Then he brought out the crusading bimonthly **Fact**, which was the first major American magazine to inveigh against U.S. involvement in Vietnam, cigarette advertising in the mass media, and Detroit's ruthless disregard for car safety (Ralph Nader was a **Fact** discovery). The intellectual community was galvanized by **Fact** and bought—devoured!—over half a million copies, despite the fact that **Fact** was not available at most newsstands (most newsdealers found it too controversial) and it was priced at a steep $1.25. But certain Very Important Persons got mad at **Fact**—including Barry Goldwater, who sued the magazine for $2 million—and it, too, was driven out of business.

Undaunted, Ginzburg rallied his forces and last year launched still a third magazine, **Avant-Garde**, which he describes as "a pyrotechnic, futuristic bimonthly of intellectual pleasure." This magazine, he predicted, "will be my wildest yet, and most universally wanted."

From all indications, Ginzburg's prediction is proving correct. Although still in its infancy, **Avant-Garde** already enjoys a readership of over one million, while its growth rate is one of the phenomena of modern publishing. Newsdealers report deliveries of copies sold out within a matter of minutes. Dentists report that **Avant-Garde** is the magazine in their waiting rooms most frequently purloined. And librarians order duplicate—and even triplicate—subscriptions in order to provide replacements for worn-out copies (and perhaps to obtain fresh copies for their own personal delectation). Everywhere, citizens who are normally upright, respectable, and law-abiding are being tempted to beg, borrow, or steal copies of **Avant-Garde**, the most spellbinding and desperately sought-after magazine in America today.

What makes **Avant-Garde** such a tutti-frutti frappe of a magazine? Why is it in such insane demand? How does it differ from other magazines? The answer is threefold:

First, **Avant-Garde** is such rollicking great fun. Each issue really socks it to you with uproarious satire, irreverent interviews, madcap cartoons, ballsy editorials, deliberately biased reportage, demoniacal criticism, x-ray profiles, supernova fiction, and outrageous ribaldry. From cover to cover, **Avant-Garde** is one big bawdyhouse of intellectual pleasure.

Second, **Avant-Garde** stones readers with its mind-blowing beauty. It brings to the printed page a transcendental new kind of high. This is achieved through a combination of pioneering printing methods and the genius of Herb Lubalin, who is **Avant-Garde**'s art director (and, incidentally, America's foremost graphic designer). In just the first few months of its existence, **Avant-Garde** has won more awards for design excellence than any other magazine in the world.

Third, **Avant-Garde** captivates readers with articles that have something to *say*. They're more than just filler between advertisements, as in most other magazines. Perhaps the best way to prove this is to list for you the kinds of articles **Avant-Garde** prints:

Will the Vote for 18-Year-Olds Move America to the Left?

Caught in the Act—An evening with New York's scandalous Orgy-and-Mystery Theater.

The Secret Plans of Leading Tobacco Companies to Market Marijuana—If, as, and when pot prohibition is lifted.

Yevgeny Yevtushenko's Epic Poem in Defense of Dr. Spock

Living High on "The Hog Farm"—A visit to America's most successful hippie *kibbutz*.

Pre-Mortem—At **Avant-Garde**'s invitation, 28 celebrities (including Art Buchwald, Harry Golden, Woody Allen, and Gore Vidal) dictate their own obituaries.

"In Gold We Trust"—A satire on America's changing spiritual values, by Dan ("How to Be a Jewish Mother") Greenburg.

London's "Theatre of Eros"

The Case of Hitler's Missing Left Testicle—A round-table discussion on an intriguing detail of Russia's recently released autopsy of Der Fuhrer. (Satirist Paul Krassner speculates that "It's probably alive and well in Argentina." Philosopher Larry Josephson contends that "Hitler just wanted to prove that he was a consistent right-winger.")

My Son, the Revolutionary—A study of the family backgrounds of young American radicals.

Flowers of the Asphalt Jungle—A tour of Harlem's beautiful new African boutiques.

The Love Poetry of Eugene McCarthy

Custom-Made Man—The portent of latest genetic research.

Coming Attraction—"Sex is the closest I can come to explaining the way I sing," says San Francisco rock songstress Janis Joplin. "I want to do it till it isn't there any more."

Has LBJ Secretly Converted to Catholicism?—A mass of circumstantial evidence.

Live Wires—A report on Liberation News Service (LNS), the Underground Press Syndicate (UPS), and Intergalactic World Brain (IWB), the three supercharged wire services that supply news to the nation's 200 underground newspapers.

R. Buckminster Fuller's Plan for a Floating City in Tokyo Bay

Fractured Hip—A collection of hilarious malapropisms by squares attempting to sound ultra-cool.

Free-Style Olympics—A report on the movement to revive Olympics in the nude.

Allen Ginsberg's Script for a New Film by Charlie Chaplin

The Pedernales River Baptism-a-thon: A Fugs Happening

1968 newsprint advertisement advocating Ralph Ginzburg's right to publish *Eros* magazine.

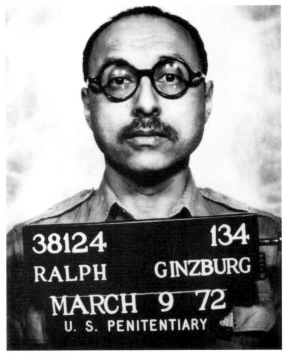

Actual 1972 US penitentiary mug shot taken when Ginzburg began his sentence for sending pornographic material through the mail. *Courtesy Unit Editions.*

and wanted magazines of the twentieth century." The text cites the spat with Goldwater as a publishing milestone: "The intellectual community was galvanized by *Fact* and bought—devoured—over half a million copies, despite the fact that *Fact* was not available at most newsstands. . . . But certain Very Important Persons got mad at *Fact*, including Barry Goldwater, who sued the magazine for $2 million, and it, too, was driven out of business."

Following paragraphs that were certain to seize liberal-left sympathies, the narrative continued: "Undaunted, Ginzburg rallied his forces and last year launched still a third magazine, *Avant Garde*. . . . Although still in its infancy, *Avant Garde* already enjoys a readership of over one million, while its growth rate is one of the phenomena of modern publishing."

At the time, "Wanted" captured my heart, mind, and wallet. And what sealed the deal was not such stories as "The Secret Plans of Leading Tobacco Companies to Market Marijuana," "Allen Ginsberg's Script for a New Film by Charlie Chaplin," or "The Case of Hitler's Missing Left Testicle," but rather the following answer to the rhetorical "What makes *Avant Garde* such a tutti-frutti frappé of a magazine?"

"*Avant Garde* stones its readers with its mind-blowing beauty. It brings to the printed page a transcendental new kind of high. This is achieved through a combination of pioneering printing methods and the genius of Herb Lubalin, who is *Avant Garde*'s art director (and, incidentally, America's foremost graphic designer)."

For a teenager (me) with the ambition to be an art director, reading that paragraph (and seeing the magazine) was such music to my eyes that I followed through with a subscription. And took heed of Ginzburg's suggestion to "sit back and prepare to receive your first copy of the most wanted, arresting, and rewarding magazine in America today (and the only one put out by a publisher with real conviction)."

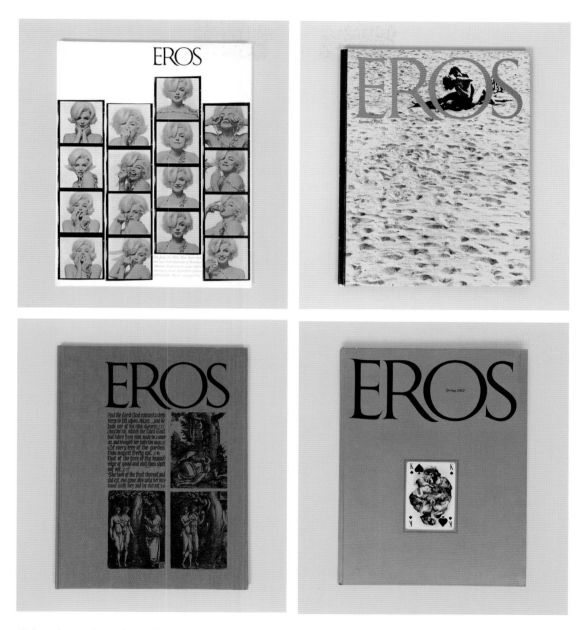

All four editions of *Eros*, designed by Herb Lubalin. Today the magazine would be considered elegantly tame. Courtesy *Unit Editions*.

THE DARK SIDE OF DESIGN

AN ONLINE EXHIBITION HOSTED BY THE MUSEUM OF MODERN ART EXPLORED THE FREQUENT INTERSECTION OF DESIGN AND VIOLENCE.

Cognitive scientist Steven Pinker's book *The Better Angels of Our Nature* posits that despite new high-tech methods of destruction and ongoing global conflicts, the world has overall become a less-violent place. But this claim didn't seem completely right to Paola Antonelli, a senior curator at the Museum of Modern Art, and to Jamer Hunt, the director of Parsons's graduate program in transdisciplinary design. They instead believed that designers, intentionally or unintentionally, may have simply helped violence mutate into other, new forms.

Pinker's book inspired Antonelli and Hunt to curate *Design and Violence,* a hybrid "exhibition" and critical forum that has been hosted online by MoMA for the last eighteen months. This week the museum published a book of the same title that addresses the impact of design on everything from shooting targets to lethal-injection drug cocktails. The project looks specifically at changes that occurred after 2001—a watershed year for the perception of violence in the United States.

The project is organized around four different themes—Hack, Control, Trace, and Annihilate—and the website includes essays from critics and experts from outside the design world, including NPR's Jad Abumrad, novelist William Gibson, and media mogul Arianna Huffington.

The "Hack" section considers nonviolent objects, such as the mundane box cutter, that have been repurposed for violent ends, regardless of the designer's original intention. Similarly, 3-D printers have been used to make guns. But, as Antonelli noted, 3-D printers also prompt us to think about how open-source design can subvert subtler forms of violence such as governmental control of intellectual property. Sometimes hacked objects can be transformed from neutral to beneficial, Antonelli said, as when protesters in Istanbul's Taksim Square used cleaning-product containers to spray milk into their eyes to minimize the effects of tear gas.

The curators said in an email that they noticed some surprising responses to the essays that appeared on the website. For one, people were more outraged about designs that engender forms of violence toward animals than toward humans. An analysis of Temple Grandin's serpentine ramp, designed to make the slaughter of cattle more humane, remains the most-discussed post on the site. "People were far less affected by the design of the lethal-injection cocktail, for example, even when we invited Ricky Jackson, an exonerated Death Row prisoner, to write a very eloquent response," they said.

Antonelli recalled one particularly memorable reply from a commenter suffering from chronic pain who defended a speculative project by Julijonas Urbonas called Euthanasia Coaster. The metaphoric roller coaster was conceptually designed to humanely kill its passengers after offering a range of experiences, from euphoria to thrill, from tunnel vision to a loss of consciousness. Hunt and Antonelli said this kind of audience engagement is central to the project and wouldn't have been possible in a more traditional museum setting, which remains the standard of validation for critics. Design and Violence's online hybrid form allowed the curators to "embrace ambiguity and even consider the necessity of violence, or at least its inescapable connection to design and life," Antonelli said.

H IS FOR HILLARY

WHEN MRS. CLINTON UNVEILED HER CAMPAIGN LOGO, IT WAS CONTROVERSIAL AT FIRST BUT BECAME A POWERFUL BRAND.

The growing slate of 2016 presidential candidates had barely had a chance to announce their campaigns before a new contender entered the fray, only to prove immediately divisive. The guilty party? Hillary Clinton's new logo, a blue-and-red *H* with a bold arrow as the crossbar.

Since anything to do with Hillary raises red (and blue) flags, critics assumed that the logo must be packed with symbolism. So, left-wingers were displeased that the arrow is red and points to the right, while right-wingers were annoyed that, when reversed, the arrow points left. Not since the Soviets ideologically censored art for geographical orientation—things facing West were forbidden—has the mere direction of anything been so disparaged. But that doesn't mean Hillary's logo should be given a free pass. The folks at FedEx, Tag Heuer, Amazon, and at least a dozen other corporations are justifiably upset because they have arrows in their logos, too—and how many arrows can the market bear? (Incidentally, the Nazi Stormtroopers' (SA) logo contained an *S* that turned into an arrow, but don't judge all arrows on a few rotten applications.)

As far as visual tropes go, the *H* owes its issues partly to its dubious alphabetic predecessors. Napoleon was one of the first autocrats to use a single initial, an *N*, as a monogram. Benito Mussolini's *M* was monumentalized through sculpture and distributed to his followers on badges of allegiance. The single initial implies a noblesse oblige—or as Superman's *S* implies, a kind of omniscient superpower. However, leaders in the United States of America are neither absolute rulers nor deities when referred to by initials: The shorthand names of FDR, JFK, and LBJ weren't imposed from the top so much as they were democratically adopted by their constituents.

Then came *W*: George W. Bush had a problem with his dynastic last name and needed to distinguish father from son without resorting to lineage numerals (apart from the number of the presidency itself). As it happened, W evolved into a popular nickname, but I can't imagine

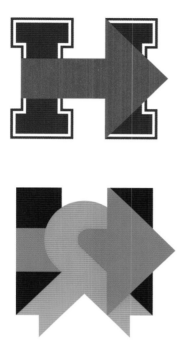

The *H* with right pointing arrow was designed by Michael Bierut with the idea it would be adapted to various constituencies.

Hillary wanting people calling her H, or even HRC, which sounds too much like a bank.

During his presidential campaign, Barack Obama's logo signaled a paradigm shift in the single-initial trope. The mnemonic *O* was consistent with the overall modernity of his entire branding style. Or maybe his image-makers realized Obama had a unique problem having the first foreign-sounding name on a major party's ticket. Using the *O* was one way to avoid spelling out Barack Hussein Obama ad infinitum. Not to mention, the *O* is the comfort food of letters; it suggests openness, opportunity, and [h]onesty. Its use during the 2008 and 2012 campaigns allowed for thematic versatility and inclusion, since various policy-centric symbolic graphic elements could fit neatly within the open letter.

Hillary's *H* is not Obama's *O*. Her arrow is not as subtle, for instance, as the arrow hidden in the negative space embedded in the FedEx logo. Rather, it's heavy-handed, which is perhaps the point. The *H* implies power. Just using the name Hillary is friendly, but much too informal for a presidential candidate. Hillary's *H* bridges the gap with its heft.

Jennifer Kinon is responsible for adapting the *H* for targeted voters, institutions, and even holidays. Courtesy Hillary Clinton Campaign.

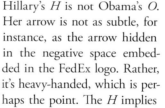

So let's look at this logo with perspective. It's already getting more attention than the bland Ted Cruz and Rand Paul logos because "H-Arrow" is the mark of a real brand. A brand conveys a story, while a label simply identifies. If the "H-Arrow" lasts through the post-convention period, it may grow on people like the Verizon logo, which survives being fundamentally ugly because nobody cares as long as they get proper customer service. If Hillary's policies live up to her promise, then the logo will follow suit. At this point, it's too early to tell, given that the campaign will last another year and a half and bring forth many other logos, signs, and slogans. The *H* may be just a placeholder, but if not, remember: logos don't win elections.

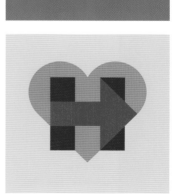

WHAT ELSE SUCKS ABOUT DONALD TRUMP? HIS BRANDING

THE FORMER REPUBLICAN FRONT-RUNNER'S IDENTITY IS AWFUL. BUT HIS SUPPORTERS DO NOT CARE.

Donald Trump's typography is a lot like Trump himself: full of attitude yet devoid of character.

For all his expertise in self-promotion—and Trump is nothing if not a masterful self-promoter—he has shown disdain for typography and branding. He favors grandiose letterforms of the sort personal injury lawyers might use, and he would do well to embrace the work of the late German type designer Georg Trump, who is no relation but prefigured the Donald with his strong typefaces. He created seventeen typefaces with names like Mauritius, Signum, and City, which was the basis for the IBM logo Paul Rand designed in 1955.

Alas, it seems the leading GOP candidate for president is contemptuous of typographic acuity and design literacy. In his book *Trump University Branding 101*, the tycoon offers the briefest discussion of managing logos and writes, "You do not need a graphic design house to develop your logo." He goes on to say, "Ideally, your logo should be unique."

Yes, one's logo should be unique. But unique is not a substitute for smart. Something can be uniquely brilliant or uniquely awful. Trump's typography is uniquely arrogant.

His campaign branding is simultaneously bold and bland, and completely uninspired. This comes as no surprise, because Trump has never shown the slightest inclination toward tasteful iconography. His history of terrible typography started with his first major development, Trump Tower. He plastered his name over the entryway in a heavy slab-serif typeface called Stymie Bold. The original Stymie, designed by Morris Fuller Benton in 1931, exemplifies a popular genre of updated

nineteenth-century slabs called Egyptian, known for their bold, blocky serifs. The typeface family was initially conceived in homage to Napoleon's 1798 Egyptian campaign, which prompted a curious worldwide craze for all things Egyptian.

It's unclear whether Trump chose Stymie out of an affinity for Napoleon or because a similar typeface called Rockwell, designed in 1934, was not angular enough to represent the flagship saw-toothed bronze skyscraper bearing his name. Whatever the reason, the dramatic thirty-four-inch-high brass Trump Tower logo marked a preference for "look at me" Stymie, which Trump would use on everything from hotels and casinos to his private jet. His choice of business typography is not fly-by-night or shady, but it is stereotypical and clichéd—the kind of font a Cadillac salesman might have on his business card or a financial advisor might place on letterhead.

Eventually, though, slab serifs may have been perceived as too plebeian for his luxury brands. So the Trump name received various typographic makeovers to express wealth and exclusivity, most vividly illustrated by the Trump Network Shield, a faux-heraldic crest, replete with regal arm and hand holding the Trump family spear.

Certain typefaces have come to express status. And although Trump's choices may not win any art school design competitions, his current serif typeface, Trajan, exudes all the attributes of imperial Roman letterforms and is named after the Trajan column, implying classical elegance and heritage. So when juxtaposed with the faux-heraldic Trump Network Shield, the idea of empire is implicit. As the Donald proclaimed in *Trump University Branding 101*: "The Trump brand includes many diverse products and services. However, the typeface and presentation of the Trump name remain constant." The Trump name further satisfies another *Branding 101* precept: "As a practical matter, your name must be pronounceable, not only in your country but in any others in which you might do business."

But when it comes to politics, Trump has decided to go for a far less Napoleonic aesthetic. For his presidential campaign, his typography is as quiet as he is loud. Actually a slew of Trump logo parodies circulating on the web, including those in which the American flag is wittily designed to resemble his famous comb-over, are far cleverer than the surprisingly subdued setting of the Donald's last name against a solid navy-blue background. The type is bold, but serifs are eliminated in favor of a sans serif similar to Franklin Gothic, while his slogan "Make America Great Again," possibly in Gill Sans, is garnished with five discreet stars. It is no frills and no thrills, which has certain advantages.

With so much attention paid to logos this early in the campaign, criticism of his logo is not something the Donald has to grapple with. Of course, he has a talent for stirring up controversy without making another typographical gaffe.

SECTION

–

02

GRAPHIC DESIGN (SOMETIMES) TRIGGERS CHANGE

GRAPHIC DESIGN (SOMETIMES) TRIGGERS CHANGE

—

DESIGNERS (AND THEIR DESIGNS) HAVE CONTRIBUTED TO CONSEQUENTIAL SHIFTS IN LANGUAGE, STYLES, AND FASHIONS. ALDUS MANUTIUS IS APT BECAUSE HIS STATUS AS AN EARLY PRINTER AND HIS INTRODUCTION OF ITALICS TO THE WESTERN WRITTEN LANGUAGE HAD SUCH CONSEQUENCE. GERMAN LOGO DESIGNER WILHELM DEFFKE MAY NOT BE AS LARGE A FIGURE AS ALDUS, BUT HE INTRODUCED SIMPLIFIED CORPORATE IDENTITY TO INDUSTRY AND, DURING THE PROCESS, INFLUENCED THE LIKES OF PAUL RAND, WHO HELPED CHANGE ATTITUDES AMONG BUSINESS LEADERS ABOUT GRAPHIC DESIGN. CHAIN REACTIONS ARE OFTEN CAUSED BY CHANGE, AND WHILE DESIGNING TOMBSTONES, BIBLES, STAMPS, AND FOOD PACKAGING MAY SEEM DISCONNECTED, ONE THING OFTEN LEADS TO ANOTHER.

THE VISIONARY BEHIND ITALICS

RENAISSANCE-ERA PRINTING INNOVATOR ALDUS MANUTIUS PIONEERED TYPE INNOVATIONS AND ENGINEERED THE PREDECESSOR TO THE PAPERBACK.

Aldus Manutius is not a household name in the same way that his predecessor by a few decades, the printing-press visionary Johannes Gutenberg, is. Yet by all accounts Manutius (1455–1515) was the greatest Venetian scholar-printer of the Italian Renaissance. He brought "portable" books to the literate masses. He was the first to print the major Greek classics and to introduce italic type. Now, on the five hundredth anniversary of his death, the communications pioneer is being remembered at the Grolier Club's "Aldus Manutius: A Legacy More Lasting Than Bronze" from February 25 to April 25, which is exhibiting 145 of the printer's rare, influential works.

The phrase "more lasting than bronze," says the exhibit's curator, G. Scott Clemons, comes from Horace's *Odes*, Book 3, Ode 30:

I have finished a monument more lasting than bronze

and loftier than the Pyramid's royal pile,

one that no wasting rain, no furious north wind

can destroy, nor the countless

chain of years and the ages' flight.

Clemons explains how he "borrowed" the sentiment for the retrospective "not only because [Manutius'] own accomplishments warrant such lofty poesy," he says, "but also because Horace was one of the earliest books printed by Manutius in his revolutionary italic type and octavo format." Several copies of the book are on exhibit in the Grolier Club, including one open to this very ode.

Manutius was a supreme innovator who transformed the hallmarks of literacy. It was due to his editions that the works of Virgil, Horace, and Dante became available to a wide audience. Manutius oversaw the typographic innovation of Francesco Griffo's Aldine (or italic) type, which was used by nearly all editions out of Manutius's Aldine Press, an operation that predated but was similar to modern commercial publishing houses. Many of the books in this exhibition were originally collected by Jean Grolier, a patron of the press who amassed an historic collection before he died in 1565.

This is not the Grolier Club's first Manutius exhibit: the organization, which was founded in 1884 by New York bibliophiles, mounted a show on the printer in 1994 ("Learning From the Greeks: An Exhibition Commemorating the 500th Anniversary of the Founding of the Aldine Press"), timed to coincide with the first publication of the Aldine Press in 1494. The early publications showcased there continue to play an important role in the club's current exhibition.

This time around, the club compasses a larger timeframe and emphasizes Manutius's grander heritage. "'A Legacy More Lasting Than Bronze' tells the story of how his innovations in typography, book design, publication, and distribution continue to influence the world of the book to this day," Clemons says. To watch the printed book being reimagined in the exhibit through the beauty of these ambitiously hand-printed volumes is visually striking. It's also a rare opportunity: of the 145 items included, 135 are privately owned and have never before been exhibited, and may never be again.

The "Dolphin and Anchor" printer's mark for Aldus Manutius represents his motto, "Festina lente" (Hurry up slowly).

"We see the lasting influence of Manutius primarily in type design and book design," Clemons says. The exhibit includes several seminal works—some in spectacular bindings, printed on vellum instead of paper, adorned with woodcuts or other decorations, or illuminated, blurring the line between the printed word and art. Included is the first book printed in Manutius's new Roman type, today called Bembo. There are also early versions of the italic type and the octavo, a smaller, portable format Manutius introduced for his Latin classics in 1501, modeled on devotional books but applied by Manutius to secular texts. The octavo helped create the concept of reading as a personal pleasure and is a direct ancestor of today's paperbacks.

Ultimately the retrospective seeks to show how Manutius's developments in typography and book design—which improved the ability of a new technology to capture, preserve, and transmit human knowledge—resonate with today's mediums. Says Clemons: "The paradigm shift of Manutius's day has much to teach us as we go through yet another paradigm shift in the twenty-first century to communicating through an electronic platform."

NUMER-0-TYPOLOGY

NUMBERS CHANGED THE WORLD AND ZERO CHANGED NUMBERS.

Mathematics was never my strong suit. For that matter, anything involved with numbers still befuddles me to the hundredth power of ten. However, I don't have to be a Pythagoras to know that our system of Hindu-Arabic numerals was not the first (nor is it now the only) numeric system in existence. Although it does raise questions as to why our base-ten numbers are designed the way they are. And what gave Arabic numerals such an advantage over the other existing systems, anyway?

To find some answers demands plugging into the searching power of Google (which by the way was named for *googolplex* and refers to an unpronounceable high numerical value) and the insight of a gaggle of math prodigies. So to reduce this subject to a fraction of its complexity so I can fathom what I'm talking about, the following is Print's Numer-0-typelogical primer on how said Hindu-Arabic system of one to ten digits (or apices), which was introduced to Europe in the twelfth century by the Italian mathematician Fibonacci (originally Leonardo di Pisa), reigns supreme.

In the Paleolithic era, the Ishango bone—the fibula of a baboon—might have been something like a numerical Rosetta stone. The notches on the side of the bone have suggested to mathematicians that it could have been used either as a tally system, or better yet, a kind of 150,000-year-old Texas Instruments calculator that we don't fully understand. On the whole, what separated early man from other mammals was his uncanny ability to count. "The necessity for numbers became more apparent when humans started to build their own houses, as opposed to living in caves and the like," writes David Osborn in his "History of Numbers," perhaps because building sustainable habitats required measurement.

The Egyptians used mathematics in their grand-scale building calculations around 3000 BC. Because they needed a language for computation, they created numerals extending from their hieroglyphic writing system to aid in facilitating the work. They used separate symbols for units of one, ten, one hundred, one thousand, and so on. Multiples of these values were expressed by tediously repeating the symbol as many times as needed. Out of this grew the hieratic ciphered numeric system—*hieratic* meaning "priestly" because priests were the keepers of the coded cipher. While fun to look at, it did not advance math in a forward direction.

Meanwhile, the Greek numbering system was based upon their twenty-six-letter alphabet, which derived from the Phoenicians around 900 BC. It was called the Attic system. As William H. Richardson of Wichita State University's Department of Mathematics and Statistic writes: "The Greeks borrowed some of the symbols and made up some of their own. But the Greeks were the first people to have separate symbols, or letters, to represent vowel sounds. Our own word alphabet comes from the first two letters, or numbers, of the Greek alphabet—*alpha* and *beta*." The Attic system was similar to its contemporary forms of numbering, insofar as it was based on symbols lined up in rows, requiring a lot of space to write (and actually, to carve in stone)—making spot quizzes not so spot on.

A thousand years before Europeans adopted the Hindu-Arabic numeral system, Roman numerals dominated. We still learn how to read them in school since they appear at the end of old movies. The Romans were less interested in abstract ideas than hard realities, so their numbers were evocations of power. A legacy of the Etruscan period, according to Gianni A. Sarcone at Archimedes's Laboratory online, Roman numeration is based on a biquinary system based on fives. Romans used an additive system: V + I + I = VII (7) or C + X + X + I (121), and also a subtractive system: IX (I before X = 9), XCIV (X before C = 90 and I before V = 4, 90 + 4 = 94). The numerals were used, though not for computation, until the late XVI century, and still hold a place-value in our hearts.

Early Sanskrit writings on mathematics include reported problems of trade and social dealings that involved complicated calculations. Numerals were required to address these. So, in India around 500 BC, a system was developed to represent each number from one to nine. (Zero had not been invented yet.) These became known as Arabic numerals because they spread first to Islamic nations, where they were readily adopted. But this was not the case in Europe, which was tightly bound to religious fantasies that precluded scientific enlightenment for around one thousand years. Prior to the West's eventual acceptance of Arabic numerals, counting one's fingers using a complex hand sign language was de rigeur.

Zero was the game-changer. The earliest known inscription of numerals to include the symbol for zero, writes Osborn, was a small circle that was found at the Chaturbhuja Temple at Gwalior, India, dated AD 876. "This Sanskrit inscription states that a garden was planted to produce flowers for temple worship and calculations were needed to assure they had enough flowers. Fifty garlands are mentioned (line 20), here 50 and 270 are written with zero." The mighty zero was the key that opened a door to Indian science, and the base-ten number system.

Vintage (c.1910) retail price tags using the familiar Arabic-inspired numerals.

But why did it take so long to find zero? Previously, people used math for simple calculations—namely counting. The idea of a mark signifying "nothing" was a new idea necessary for advanced calculations. With numbers one to ten it is possible to combine an infinite assortment of digits (e.g., 15987) to achieve a whole number, rather than in the Roman additive system. The West adopted the base-ten system in the twelfth century so that merchants could do business with Arab traders, and it has been essential to the Western numerical construct ever since. So that's where our numbers came from. But why do they look the way they do?

Number 1 has its roots in India. The writing of the number, thanks to the Gupta Empire, was a curved line, and the Nagari added a small circle on the left that made it look like a 9 in the Gujarati and Punjabi scripts. The Nepali had their own ideas and rotated it to the right, keeping a small circle making something akin to a top serif in the modern numeral. There is an occasional short horizontal line at the bottom that is similar to the Roman letter. Also occasionally, a little serif at the top is sometimes extended into a long upstroke.

The lineage of the **Number 2** starts with the Brahman Indians; their 2 was drawn as two horizontal lines. The Guptas' contribution was to rotate the lines at a forty-five-degree diagonal. The Nagari reduced the top line to a curve that connected to the bottom line. The numbers in tenth-century Islamic Spain were a Western variant from the Arabic-speaking world, known as Ghubar numerals. These Ghubar used a vertical bottom line, making it appear like a horizontal question mark without the dot. In the final stage of its evolution, the bottom line was returned to the horizontal position and the top line became a curve that connects to the bottom line.

The Brahmans' **Number 3** was originally written with three horizontal lines. The Guptas curved the three lines while the Nagari rotated the lines clockwise and ended each line with a slight downward stroke on the right, which over time connected with the lines below and evolved into a character that looks very much like a modern 3 with an extra stroke at the bottom. The Ghubar Arabs eliminated the extra stroke and created our modern 3.

The Brahman simplified the **Number 4**. Its four lines were made into a cross, something like a plus sign. The Sunga introduced a horizontal line on top while the Kshatrapa and Pallava streamlined the form. The Arab 4 had the early concept of the cross, made into a single stroke by connecting what scholars called the "Western" end to the "Northern" end; the "Eastern" end was finished off with a curve. Once in Europe the curve was eliminated and the number became more rectilinear, more in keeping with the Brahman cross.

Number 5 does not sync up directly with the Indian numeric system. The Nagari and Punjabi glyphs suggest a 180 degree lowercase *h*. The Ghubar devised signs that were more similar to 3 or 4 than to the number 5. However, from these characters the Europeans devised the familiar 5. (Although there is an argument that the modern symbol came from the Khmer, where the Kushana/Ândhra/Gupta numeral has an extended swirled "tail.")

Number 6 is another Brahman-derived glyph. It was commonly written in one stroke like a cursive lowercase *e* rotated 90 degrees clockwise. Evolutionarily, the top of the stroke was more curved, while the bottom squiggle was made straighter. The Ghubar Arabs dropped the part of the stroke below the squiggle. The European contribution was fairly direct, yet it did look like an uppercase *G*.

Hindus wrote their **Number 7** in one stroke as a curve that looks like an uppercase *J* vertically inverted. The western Ghubar Arabs replaced the straight line with a longer diagonal, making it more rectilinear. The European two-stroke glyph shows a horizontal upper line joined on the right side to a line extending down to the bottom-left corner.

The first century Brahman sign for **Number 8** was written in one stroke as a curve in the shape of an uppercase *H*, where the bottom part of left line and the upper portion of the right is removed: ⅃. But before this it varied: It took the shape of a single wedge, which was adopted into the Perso-Arabic tradition as ʌ (and also gave rise to the later Devanagari numeral ⌁; the alternative curved glyph existed as a variant in Perso-Arabic tradition, where it resembled the common 5).

The line of the 5 used in Indian manuscripts for 8 formed in Ghubar as a closed loop, which was the 8-shape that became adopted into European applications.

Number 9 originally resembled a question mark. The Kshatrapa, Andhra, and Gupta curved the bottom vertical line to look like a 3. The bottom stroke was elongated by the Nagari to make a circle that enclosed the 3. As the circle evolved it became bigger—then the line extended down away from the circle, though the three-like squiggle was retained. The Arabs connected the squiggle to the downward stroke at the middle and the rest was European refinement.

The **0** was symbolic of "empty," hence the terms naught or none. The concept of zero as a number rather than a symbol derives from India; in the ninth century AD, zero was treated like all numbers. Rules governing zero appeared for the first time in the Indian mathematician Bramagupta's book *The Opening of the Universe*, written in AD 628. He considers not only zero but also negative numbers and the algebraic rules for the elementary operations of arithmetic with such numbers.

Zero changed the mathematical world. Mathematics changed the entire universe. Numerals are as powerful as letters.

For House Industries, numbers are as important as letters. This is a series of Eames numerals to use as house address numbers.

A RECLUSIVE LOGO DESIGNER GETS HIS DUE

WILHELM DEFFKE, A LITTLE-KNOWN 20TH-CENTURY GERMAN DESIGNER WITH A DISTINCTIVE MINIMALIST STYLE, GETS THE SHOWCASE HE DESERVES.

By the early 1930s, German designer Wilhelm Deffke was one of the most prolific logo designers in the business, having produced nearly ten thousand corporate symbols. Yet Deffke was never a household name: like all designers who stand for a company or a brand, he didn't typically sign his work.

A hefty new monograph, *Wilhelm Deffke: Pioneer of the Modern Logo* (published by Scheidegger & Spiess and the Berlin-based Bröhan Design Foundation) is bringing Deffke some long-deserved name recognition. The 388-page tome, published in November, contains five hundred reproduced versions of Wilhelm's work on posters and commercial art, and fourteen essays expanding upon his significance. The collection champions Wilhelm as the "father of the modern logo."

In addition to being a founder, though, Deffke was a collaborator. He cofounded the Berlin advertising agency "Wilhelm Werk" in 1915 with his partner Carl Ernst Hinkefuss after a stint with the pioneer German industrial designer Peter Behrens. There, for more than thirty years, Deffke practiced the precisionist art of graphic reductionism, influencing subsequent generations to transform literal objects and characters into stark, symbolic, sometimes comical logos.

Some of Deffke's designs are still in use today, including the wittily conjoined twin geometrical figures for the cutlery giant J. A. Henckels. Another, less-popular design is Deffke's deft refinement of the ancient swastika, which one of his former assistants claimed was later usurped by the Nazis when they repurposed the symbol in 1920.

Torsten Bröhan, a gallerist, entrepreneur, and founder of the Bröhan Design Foundation, bought Deffke's estate in 2010. "I was from the first minute convinced that I had the duty to bring this avantgardistic graphic design to a broader public," he told me. At no small cost, Bröhan sought out eleven art historians and two design experts, some of them teaching at German universities, to collaborate in writing Deffke's historiography for the book and building a virtual design archive.

Bröhan says Deffke was an *einzelgänger*—a solitary, private person—so little is known about his personal life. Here's what is: Deffke attended the Kunstgewerbeschule school of applied arts in Elberfeld (today a part of Wuppertal), moved to Berlin, and worked in Peter Behrens's workshop, where he met the founding director of the Bauhaus, Walter Gropius, and the architects Adolf Meyer and Ludwig Mies van der Rohe. He particularly became close to Gropius, who, as chairman of the department of architecture at Harvard University, would swear Deffke never cooperated with the Nazis in a letter to German officials after World War II.

Contemporary typographers started copying the "Deffke Style" that characterized his work after an entire issue of Seidel's *Reklame*—a monthly review on commercial typography—was devoted to Deffke's work in 1923. "This issue brought him a recognition nationwide," Bröhan explains, but also criticism by conservative journalists and colleagues for his cutting-edge, minimalist approach. His most famous logos, including one for Vox-Schallplatten- und Sprechmaschinen-AG, a record company, and Reemtsma, a tobacco and cigarette company, exhibit his flair for spare design.

As far as Bröhan knows, the Nazis never used any advertising displays, posters, or logos designed by Deffke, though he produced some environmental and showroom advertising displays that prefigured some Nazi extravaganzas. Hitler's rise to power, indeed, was a tough time for Deffke: In 1933 he lost his position as director and professor at the Kunstgewerbeschule Magdeburg and gave up his agency in Berlin. A big commission from the British American Tobacco company gave him the financial resources to open a new agency outside the city, and "from time to time the Nazis tried to force him to cooperate with them," Bröhan notes, citing documents from his estate. "But Deffke was able to resist."

Deffke's most stunning designs in the book are perhaps previously unseen; the ones he worked on until his death in 1950 at age sixty-three. Pristinely preserved and reproduced therein, the volume comprises a valuable document championing an old face in the history of branding with new emphasis.

Series of logos c.1920s–30s designed by Wilhelm Deffke for various corporations. The swastika was designed for luck and used by different businesses.

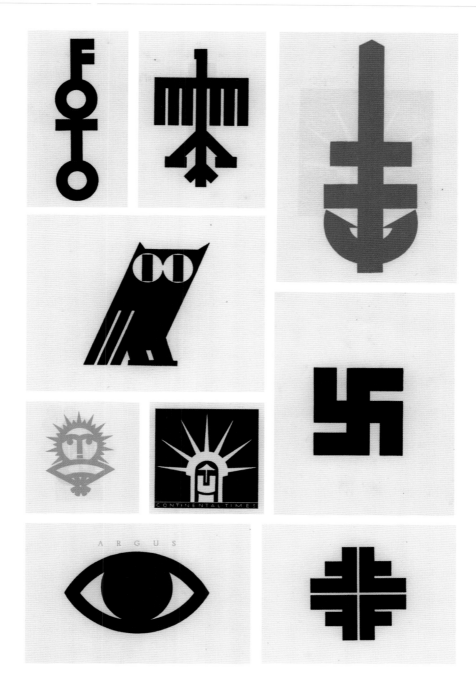

THE LOST GRAPHIC DESIGNS OF A SHORT-LIVED DEMOCRACY

HISTORY NEARLY FORGOT THE AVANT-GARDE, SOMETIMES AGITATIONAL PUBLISHING CULTURE THAT FLOURISHED IN THE REPUBLIC OF LATVIA BETWEEN WORLD WARS.

Between World War I, when the Republic of Latvia was constituted as a parliamentary democracy, and World War II, when democracy was forcibly squelched, Latvia's capitol city, Riga, hosted a thriving avant-garde publishing community. The scene produced a rich vein of books and periodicals printed in Latvian, Russian, German, and Yiddish and typographically designed using a range of Cubistic, Constructivist, Bauhaus, Futurist, Expressionistic, and Dada mannerisms of the day. Even French-inspired art nouveau and art moderne (art deco) graphic design was infused into Latvian publishing culture. All of that began to end in 1940, when the nation alternately endured occupations from the Soviets, the Nazis, and then the Soviets again.

This geographically circumscribed golden age would be mostly lost to history were it not for years of intensive sleuthing by Dr. James Howard Fraser, a type and design historian. He died in November 2013, just months before the release of his book *Publishing and Book Design in Latvia 1919-1940: A Re-discovery* (published by Neputns, Riga, and distributed in the United States by Oak Knoll Books).

While not the most excitingly titled work, this scholarly volume is an exhaustive—and, for typophiles, entertaining—account of a little-known enclave of innovation, with hundreds of reproductions of rare and beautiful books and periodicals. Anyone curious about the power of design to define moments in time and place, or fetishistically interested in old printed paper, will be fascinated by the artifacts Fraser was able to harvest from museum basements, hidden archives, and collectors' warrens. The visuals are enticing, but the range of scholarship is beyond impressive; Fraser has unearthed everything from commercial weeklies and monthlies to left-wing political journals and pamphlets to Zionist children's textbooks and illustrated storybooks from Russian, German, and Yiddish publishers.

Riga was filled with artists who have been ignored in histories of European design. They were sponges who soaked up modernist methods, sometimes mimicking and other times reinterpreting what was generated in the continent's more visible and historically recognized centers of art and design, including the USSR, Poland, Czechoslovakia, and Hungary. Still, a Latvian graphic sensibility—or Baltic style—emerged through a surfeit of large and small publications. Like most other European modern movements, its creators were smothered by oppressive Nazi decrees and Soviet Social Realist doctrines until designers were prohibited from doing anything but state-sanctioned work.

Yet before the final blow, the Riga-based Yiddish press was riding a renaissance wave. *Idishe Bilder* (Jewish Pictures), edited by, among others, Zelig Kalmanovitch, "worked at bringing the world to Yiddish-reading Jewry," Fraser wrote. "The very first issue's cover story on India's Jews is but one example." Photojournalism was the key to the paper's short-lived success. Every issue had a photographic cover, and photomontage was common inside. When war loomed, *Idishe Bilder* published a series about those countries to which Jews could flee.

The political left also made up a significant portion of avant-garde publishing, from "mild social democratic strains" to "the hardest core within the Latvian Communist Party." The design of the latter echoed the radical Russian Constructivist formats ultimately preempted by Stalin's turgid Social Realism. The most exciting of these were *Jauna Gvarde* (The New Garde, 1928), *Informators* (the Informer, 1932), and *Kreisa Fronte* (The Left Front, 1928–30), which together put the names of two unheralded artist/designers into the world: Ernests Kalis and Samuils Haskins, who designed covers and produced woodcut illustrations.

That some artifacts from the interwar period survived the subsequent political and cultural warfare is incredible. That they are documented today is due to Fraser's dogged research. Fraser, who had also authored books on the American billboard, Japanese modernism, and Czech book design, wrote clearly and precisely. His final book was a worthy use of his skills, bringing Latvia's design avant-garde out from the shadow of Europe's better-known movements.

THE DESIGNER WHO HUMANIZED CORPORATE AMERICA

PAUL RAND, A PIONEER WHO RE-ENVISIONED THE LOOK OF MEGACOMPANIES WITH WHIMSICAL, COLORFUL LOGOS AND ILLUSTRATIONS

"Visual communications of any kind . . . from billboards to birth announcements, should be seen as the embodiment of form and function: the integration of the beautiful and the useful," wrote Paul Rand (1914–1996) in 1947's *Thoughts on Design*.

It was a mantra Rand, one of America's premier mid-century modern graphic designers, lived and championed. An interpreter of European modernism, Rand helped give a playful corporate identity to major American industries and designed some of the nation's most recognizable business logos—for IBM, Westinghouse, UPS, ABC, and even Colorforms. Logos were his forte—but he also lent his minimalist style to book covers, children's book illustrations, posters, and package designs.

Now a portion of this tremendous body of work is on display at the Museum of the City of New York. "Everything is Design: The Work of Paul Rand," curated by Donald Albrecht, is Rand's first solo New York museum exhibition. For Albrecht, Rand's work presented an opportunity for the museum to explore graphic design's considerable impact on the city's visual culture. "[Rand] is one of those 'only in New York' stories of reinvention that many of us New Yorkers think makes the city tick," Albrecht says.

Rand was born in Brooklyn to two Orthodox Jewish grocers and studied, along with his twin brother, at a yeshiva. After a period spent learning about the Bauhaus and studying at the

Art Students League of New York with George Grosz, Rand went to work in advertising. As one of the youngest art directors for New York–based advertising agency Weintraub, he designed for Ohrbach's department store, El Producto cigars, and the aperitif liquor Dubonnet. He worked for Manhattan publishers Knopf, Vintage, and Pantheon creating abstract book covers and jackets, and gained a reputation with designs for blue-chip companies like IBM, Cummins Engines, Westinghouse, Morningstar, and even Enron. By 1986 he was such a star that Steve Jobs received special dispensation from Apple's sworn rival, IBM, to enlist Rand to design his post-Apple venture, the NeXT logo.

"His story helps us explore New York's creativity," Albrecht says. The show begins with a selection of his distinct magazine cover designs from the 1930s (including covers for the left-wing *Direction* and fashion-centric *Men's Apparel*), which show him adapting sophisticated European avant-garde ideas about symbolism and dislocation to American commerce at a very young age. It also includes a few examples of the European magazines he was inspired by, as well as a copy of the forward-looking American magazine *Look*. "With material this great," Albrecht says, "a big assertive curatorial viewpoint isn't needed or welcome."

The exhibit, designed by the Martin Perrin Studio, has a minimal-modern aesthetic that fits Rand's own sensibility and underscores the wide range of Rand's inventiveness. Albrecht particularly wants visitors to the museum to appreciate that art comes from the commercial, as well as the private, sphere. "Maybe that's something artists like Andy Warhol and Jeff Koons have shown us," he says, "But Rand was an early and extraordinary advocate of the concept."

For Albrecht, curating the show was a lesson in learning the power of deft design to boil complex companies down to singularly human symbols. "Rand was working during the Cold War for big corporate clients who he helped humanize and make more friendly," Albrecht says. "Like Charles and Ray Eames, he spread a bright and cheerful image of pax Americana."

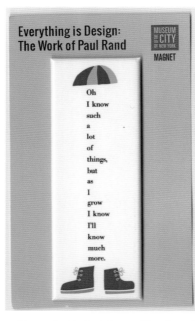

Rare advertisement for Kaiser Automobile Company for its 1951 models.

Magnet for 2015 exhibition of Rand's work at the Museum of the City of New York.

Folder used at IBM executive meetings, c.1962.

Covers of Direction magazine were Rand's laboratory.

The Graphic art of Paul Rand

Poster for a traveling exhibition of his graphic design.

RCA'S NEW TRADEMARK 1968

C.E.O. ROBERT W. SARNOFF UNDERSTOOD THE IMPORTANCE OF IDENTITY THROUGH GRAPHIC DESIGN.

On April 13, 1968, the *Saturday Review* published an essay by Robert W. Sarnoff, President and CEO of the Radio Corporation of America (RCA) on the development of the corporation's new identity and logotype. Titled "Anatomy of a New Trademark," it is an extraordinary example of how one leader of American industry, particularly in the electronic and computer fields, understood the value of good design and the role of designers in the maintenance of corporate image.

IBM, Westinghouse, General Dynamics, CBS, and others adhered to what IBM's Thomas J. Watson famously said: "Good design is good business." Less famous, perhaps, but no less eloquent is Sarnoff's more than two-thousand-word article that not only explained the rationale behind RCA's change of visual strategy almost six decades ago (the trademark that is still in use), but speaks to today's branding practices too.

Incidentally, changing the mark was not taken lightly, since RCA's original circular logotype dated from 1922 on an advertisement for the Grand Aeriola radio receiver featuring an endorsement by Guglielmo Marconi and was one of the best known American trademarks. "Anatomy" shows the intelligence necessary to ensure that the project, which took over two years, achieved a more-than-satisfactory outcome.

Sarnoff begins with a clear declaration that sets the stage for his compelling argument about why a shift in design strategy was necessary:

The public view of a corporation is a composite of millions of private impressions. It is the combined experience of all those who use its products and services or receive its visual and verbal messages. For RCA, it is the executive consulting a computer, the student using an instructional system, the housewife reading an ad, the job-hunter leafing through a company brochure. It is a mosaic or, more aptly, a television screen whose luminescent dots are constantly changing to form broad new patterns.

He continues his rationale by addressing the corporate history and future:

RCA's corporate look, exemplified by its circled initials and lightning bolt, was one of the most famous in the business world. It dated from a time when the company was devoted entirely to international wireless communications—a commitment that has continued to grow, but today accounts for only 2 percent of our total volume. The question then, was whether a design system devised for a wireless company in the 1920s could suggest the diverse operations of RCA in the changing environment of the '60s, and beyond.

RCA's 1968 logo designed by Lippincott & Margulies that replaced the RCA with the lightning bolt (page 73).

Since the entire essay is too long to reprint in this space, I've distilled the essay down to its narrative essence, which I hope retains Sarnoff's design acuity. It is encouraging that a CEO had such an enthusiastic and knowledgeable response to a corporation's identity.

Sarnoff proceeds with a description of the process itself and his own involvement:

The analysis of a corporate identity, like that of an individual personality, calls for objective, professional help. We discussed RCA's needs with several design and communications consultants. In June 1966, we engaged the firm of Lippincott & Margulies. . . . During the next eighteen months, I was involved in the project every step of the way and took special interest in its progress, for it added new insights to my own examination of the company as its new president. . . .

Lippincott & Margulies's conclusion after six months of study was that the outward face of RCA should reflect more fully its inner reality. Our corporate look should measure up to an enterprise that, in less than fifty years had advanced from its base in wireless communications to technological frontiers extending from the core of the atom to the surface of Mars. It should suggest the diversity of a corporation producing some 12,000 different products, most of which were not in existence as recently as a decade ago. . . . Our first need was a clearer concept of the scope of RCA. We drew up what, for a lack of a better term, we called a "corporate philosophy"—a basic view of the company as it is and as it should develop in the future.

For the sake of the layman and stockholder, Sarnoff pinpoints how the company has grown out of its old skin:

We started with our full corporate title, which, as someone pointed out, was reminiscent of Voltaire's remark about the Holy Roman Empire—that it was neither holy, nor Roman, nor an empire. The Radio Corporation of America remains a corporation, to be sure, but it is by no means restricted in its facilities, products, and services to the radio industry or to the American continent. The full name, furthermore, is too long and unwieldy for visual and phonetic impact. We would retain it as our legal title, but we would henceforth focus on the RCA initials, which over the years have become the public's natural way to refer to the company. . . .

For all its nostalgia, the old trademark presented several design problems. Its Roman letters were closer in spirit of the Jazz Age than to an era of space exploration. The lightning symbol, fitting enough for the early days of radio, had become more familiarly associated with the power industry than with electronics. The circle itself was not only restrictive in its effect, but sat uneasily on the rectangular forms of most of our products.

Sarnoff was a realist. Paul Rand likened a logo to a rabbit's foot. Sarnoff talks not in mystical terms but in functional ones:

Any commercial design must eventually stand the acid test of practical application. Before making a decision, therefore, we put the block letters and the other new logos to the test. We applied each of them to a selection of more than fifty products and other items. . . .

This practical demonstration made it clear that the block letters had the distinctive and flexible style we were looking for. Their clean, unique design caught the attention and held it. They could be rendered opaque, transparent, or in outline. . . . On a gleaming Spectra 70 computer or a Video-comp typesetter, the mark not only measured up to the product but enhanced it.

After all the prep work, the decision to make the change was made, and Sarnoff understood it had to be in keeping with tradition yet be forward-looking too:

By late 1967, we were ready for the immense task of putting the new system into effect, and we created a corporate position to supervise the effort and keep the new look up to date. . . .

The corporate style must also be translated into the design of office interiors, research centers, and manufacturing plants. To a company's employees, customers, and suppliers—and to the public that simply passes by—these are often the most visible and memorable expressions of corporate style.

We were especially encouraged by the enthusiastic response of many creative people—product designers, advertising artists, copywriters, and architects—who felt that the new style would liberate and revitalize their efforts to communicate the dynamism and diversity of the company.

Sarnoff's kicker reads like the goal of every designer, identity consultant, and CEO:

"For me, however, the most significant comment of all came in a letter from an electronics engineer of another firm who had just seen one of our new ads. 'RCA', he wrote, 'looks like the kind of company that I would like to work for'."

How Television Got Its Electronic "Eyes"

As revolutionary as airplanes without propellers —that's how much electronic television differs from the earlier mechanical television!

Whirling discs and motors required for mechanical television were not desirable for home receivers. Pictures blurred and flickered.

But now, thanks to RCA research, you will enjoy all-electronic television, free from all mechanical restrictions—"movie-clear" television with the same simplicity and efficiency of operation as your home radio receiver.

Such "let's make it better" research goes into everything produced by RCA. Scientists and engineers at RCA Laboratories are constantly seeking new and better ways of harnessing the unbelievable forces of nature . . . for mankind's greater benefit and enjoyment.

Electronic television is but one example of the great forward strides made possible by RCA research —opening the way for who knows what new miracles of tomorrow?

When you buy an RCA radio or phonograph or television set or any RCA product, you get a great satisfaction . . . enjoy a unique pride of ownership in knowing that you possess one of the finest instruments of its kind that science has yet achieved.

Dr. V. K. Zworykin, Associate Research Director, and E. W. Engstrom, Director of Research at RCA Laboratories, examining the Iconoscope or television "eye"—developed in RCA Laboratories for the all-electronic television system.

RADIO CORPORATION of AMERICA

PIONEERS IN PROGRESS RCA

1947 advertisement showing how RCA was branching out into a multimedia corporation that had outgrown its lightning-bolt logo.

REVISITING THE WORK OF ONE OF THE TWENTIETH CENTURY'S BEST AD MEN

ART DIRECTOR GEORGE LOIS HELPED MAKE SOME OF THE TRANSFORMATIVE ADVERTISEMENTS OF THE MODERN COMMERCIAL ERA.

Until the late 1950s, American advertising had been plagued by work that the writer Aldous Huxley referred to as possessing "a moderate excellence . . . not too good, but sufficiently striking." In other words, these ads weren't bad, just acceptable; they were mediocre despite the awards they won. But then in the '60s came the so-called "Creative Revolution," helmed by a new breed of daring Jewish, Italian, and Greek American art directors. Armed with artistic intelligence, conceptual sophistication, and theatrical flair, they were gung ho about going head-to-head with the industry's white, Anglo-Saxon old guard. And their work paid off.

The 1960s was a period informed by the Civil Rights movement, the burgeoning women's liberation movement, the Vietnam War, and other shifts during the turbulent, roller-coaster decade that altered America forever. These changes also served as the underpinning for some of the best ad men of the time. But by the 1970s, the "big idea" creative agencies were winning their share of awards and accolades too, for commercials that won over print and TV audiences with their wit, not just their sales pitches.

But what set the '70s apart from the previous decade? After all, much of the ad work done in the '70s drew from the same cleverness and creativity that first sprang up in the '60s—a time when unconventional became memorable, and memorable meant capturing a substantial market share of hearts and minds.

"You're some tomato.
We could make beautiful Bloody Marys together.
I'm different from those other fellows."

"I like you, Wolfschmidt.
You've got taste."

Wolfschmidt Vodka has the touch of taste that marks genuine old world vodka. Wolfschmidt in a Bloody Mary is a tomato in triumph.
Wolfschmidt brings out the best in every drink. GENERAL WINE AND SPIRITS CO., NEW YORK 22. MADE FROM GRAIN, 80 OR 100 PROOF. PRODUCT OF U.S.A.

The most progressive liquor ad of its day, 1960, produced by PKL.

It was true that by the '70s, "watching TV, you would see a damn good TV spot every night," said George Lois, the legendary art director and a pioneer of the Big Idea, who helped emancipate advertising from the hard sell. But as ads grew more creative and alluring, said Lois, "the more the establishment agencies, including Ogilvy, tried to sell advertising as a science, not an art." In other words, by the '70s, the industry was increasingly driven by psychological research and market testing, which contributed to large-scale shifts in product loyalty.

Another seismic shift brought on by the Creative Revolution was the introduction of the writer and artist/designer as a team. Lois, who was trained as a designer, often served in both roles.

UniRoyal's vinyl, Naugahyde, became a cultural icon after Lois created the mythical Nauga species, made into an ugly doll that shed its skin for the benefit of sitting (on a chair). Surprisingly, some people thought it was a real leather-baring creature.

Royal Air Maroc's "I'm off on the road to Morocco . . . again" ad featured Dorothy Lamour thirty years after her costarring role with Bob Hope and Bing Crosby in *The Road to Morocco*—a memorable way to put an unknown airline on everyone's lips.

In Off Track Betting's NYBets ads, Lois renamed the one-time horse betting salons to sound like "NY Mets." He also hired celebrities, including Frank Sinatra, Carol Channing, Jackie Gleason, and Bob Hope to wear the NYBets shirts in wonderfully surprising testimonial photos.

Cutty Sark's defiant "Don't Give Up the Ship" ad encouraged customers not to switch brands—and convinced Cutty not to scuttle its famous label.

Lois produced the boxer Rubin "Hurricane" Carter's campaign for a new trial following his wrongful murder conviction as a series of *New York Times* spot ads with headlines like "Counting today I have sat in prison 3,135 days for a crime I did not commit," and "When I was sentenced to 197 years in prison, even my father felt that if a jury found me guilty, then I must be guilty." Each ad was signed, "Rubin Hurricane Carter, No. 45475, Trenton State Prison." Lois's campaign enlisted dozens of celebrities, from Bob Dylan to Burt Reynolds, to advocate for a new trial. (Carter was released in 1985.)

Though some of Lois's best work came in the '80s and '90s, many of the 1970s ads for which he served as art director represent a spectrum of work that helped define the decade—the kind of work Huxley called "impressive, haunting and fascinating in [its] own right."

Lois's *Esquire* covers were journalistic events, August 1968.

MAGAZINES ARE RAD— WITH THE RIGHT DESIGN

THEY JUST NEED WIT, HUMOR, AND A GOOD ZINGER IDEA TO SEDUCE THE READER.

Great magazine covers once held pride of place in the home—certainly in my home. They were social and intellectual status symbols. And among them, ninety-two covers that George Lois created for *Esquire* from 1962 to 1972 stand above almost all others.

Lois, one of advertising's "creative revolutionaries," was the sole magazine cover designer for one of the most influential publications at a time when the public relied almost exclusively on magazines for news and views. A striking *Esquire* cover would be as talked about over lunch or dinner as a segment of *Last Week Tonight* might be now. Covers critiqued and defined the cultural and political moment—and were usually ahead of that moment. Even in the Internet age, Lois's work still has much to teach us.

Two of his most well-known covers are courageous and, therefore, unforgettable for the baby boomer generation. Both featured prize fighters: Sonny Liston as Santa Claus for the Christmas issue in 1963, and Muhammad Ali as the martyr St. Sebastian five years later. Both were charged commentaries: they addressed common fears that many white Americans felt toward black men, one hundred years after the Civil War. Yet the incredibly ironic way in which Lois presented them—one as a lily-white holiday icon, the other as a martyr to his belief that the Vietnam war was unjust—forced people to reassess the consequences of racial prejudice in the United States. Readers of the liberal-leaning magazine anticipated Lois's brash commentaries, and those of us maturing into adulthood received them as an antiestablishment rebuke of the mainstream. Even now, as they hang in the MoMA design gallery, these oversized magazine graphics still provoke a sense of unease.

Just recently, Lois found a long-lost cover for the November 1970 issue that was rejected prior to publication by his editor, who feared an advertiser backlash should *Esquire* publish it. It featured Aunt Jemima, the famous grinning product mascot, wearing a Black Panther beret, threateningly holding a meat cleaver under the headline "Lord love de Panthers!" The cleaver was a reference to Eldridge Cleaver, the Black Panther Party leader, who would in 1978 write *Soul on Ice*, capturing the interest of black and white radicals. Aunt Jemima, of course, was at the time the friendly mascot for the servile antebellum black woman.

In light of the racial struggles going on today, the power of these covers' persuasion serves as a model for how magazines should be conceived and designed today. Unorthodox cover designs are even more important to the survival of traditional print magazines now that digital platforms and products are pushing them into the margins. As long as print magazines are still viable—and if the magazine racks can be believed, they are—Lois insists that "bold, visually defined Big Idea magazine covers are essential to leap out and grab you by the throat." He says the continual barrage of images on our devices means print magazine covers should be "economic in form, big in idea, and understood at a glance," to compete with digital publications. "Most are not," he notes.

The lemmingesque cover designs today make it hard to discern one magazine from another, and even one genre from another. Among the common eyesores are those pesky coverlines announcing a magazine's contents. Like kudzu vines, coverlines climb, coil, and strangle cover art, reducing the main image to a backdrop. This is not design. It's stuffing a package with a packing manifest in an attempt to be relevant to new readers who might otherwise spend their mag-reading time online. Perhaps it has to do with attention deficit disorder, but more likely it is the publishers' insecurity owing to intense competition for time and attention. They don't know how to grab their reader, so they promote everything and hope something sticks.

Lois's covers underscore an era when magazine covers could actually influence the public's mind in the same way startling wartime posters could. Even though *Esquire* rejected the Aunt Jemima cover, the fact he felt confident presenting it is indicative of more courageous times.

Lois's cover probably would be published today, almost certainly online and almost certainly not by *Esquire,* whose covers long ago moved from social commentary to entertainment and fashion. With few exceptions, most print covers now do little more than billboard a publication's contents. Other than *The New Yorker,* which continues to reject coverlines for a single, sometimes acerbic illustration, only indie magazines avoid junking up their fronts. The majority of digital magazine covers are basically homepages with links to features. Now magazines attempt to "sell" all content just in case there might be one or two themes that will attract a buyer.

Although the presumed uproar over Lois's lost cover (inspired by a fiery James Baldwin article on black revolution) never had a chance to materialize, its is clear from the image that sparks would have flown. And its persuasive power would have had as much to do with its large-scale format as its big idea. Magazines were bigger in size and heft than today, and as miniposters on the newsstand and coffee table, these covers had palpable allure. Even magazines that were not overtly political—like *Holiday*, *Show*, *Vogue*, *Fortune*, *Look*, and *Life*—sported startling graphics, typography, and photography.

There is little comparable in the digital space to Lois's historic magazine covers. Screens are getting smaller and more individual than public. Magazines make a virtue of catering to personal tastes, so that even an argument about the cover is less possible. Digital media is all about reduction, and so many once-fertile design platforms, including record covers and book jackets, have shrunk to one-inch icons.

I am not suggesting that analog magazines do not stand a chance over the next decade. Publishers trying to combine print and digital continue to grapple with how to retain integrity between media while investing in brand consistency. Digital and analog may have the same basic content, but their approaches are inevitably different. The fact that digital magazines, including covers, can be animated in any number of ways allows for myriad applications of type and image, color and sound.

But let's stick with print magazines here, as one segment of popular messaging. Part of the beauty of great magazine covers, like great cartoons by Goya, Grosz, and Steadman, is they outlast the relevance of the related content. Readers still want to take pride in their magazines, and having consistently striking covers is part of the calculus for success. In addition to the overt message, covers like Lois's tacitly signal confident exuberance, authority, and uniqueness. If more magazines adopted these qualities, they might just give the new tech a run for the money—at least for a while.

Esquire

NOVEMBER 1970
PRICE $1

THE MAGAZINE FOR MEN

Lord love de Panthers!

(How about you? See page 68)

This cover comp Lois designed in 1970 was never published. But more than 110 equally powerful ones appeared month after month on *Esquire*.

DESIGNING A REALLY BIG BOOK

TRANSLATING THE WORD INTO PROSE DEMANDED SOME PRETTY FERVENT DESIGNERS.

The Ten Commandments were revealed to Moses on Mt. Sinai (Exodus 20–23), along with a miscellaneous set of laws conventionally called the "book of the covenant," also referred to as "stone tablets," which God had inscribed. And so it was written, and so it begat Judeo-Christian typographic design, which continues in various forms to this day.

Granted, this is a rather condensed and simplified account, but hey, we have limited space to chart the design evolution of religious messages—and little was written in the Good Book about graphic design.

For hundreds of years scribes laboriously penned biblical tracts and elaborately illuminated many of them (think *Book of Kells*). In the mid-1450s Gutenberg issued the first "43-line Bible," the first Western book to be printed with a moveable type press, triggering the greatest communications revolution for hundreds of years to follow (until St. Steve Jobs). Gutenberg's Mainz Bible looked similar to a hand-scribed manuscript, but soon text types would take precedence and then religious missives reached millions.

By the nineteenth century countless bibles, psalters, hymnals, pamphlets, and other spiritual messages from, by, and about the Lord were published the world over. Late-nineteenth-century examples, like the English variety shown here, were typographically and illustratively conservative, using existing typefaces and engraved illustrations. There were, however, a number of ecclesiastical typefaces and letterforms, Gothic in look and feel, which signify the Christian aesthetic. And these letterforms, depending on where they are found, suggest either the spiritual or hellfire-damnation qualities of religious messaging.

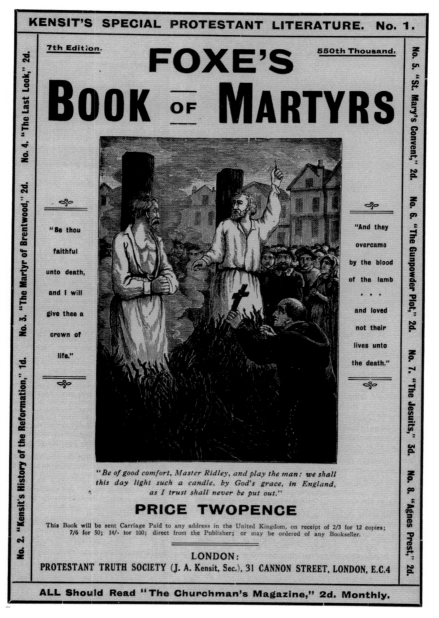

There has always been a solemn convention for designing religious, especially Judeo-Christian, publications, prayer books, and psalters. But even within those parameters, there was room for variations of type and both hellraising and heaven-praising illustrations.

Yet some designers, hearing the call, and not content to leave well enough alone even in religious precincts, have taken it as their mission to redesign—and perhaps modernize—the Bible and ancillary materials. Who said the Word had to be somber or dark (think Gustav Dore's engravings)?

In 1973 Bradbury Thompson, an alumnus of Washburn College, designed the *Washburn College Bible,* "the most thorough typographic reassessment of the Bible since Gutenberg." Thompson increased legibility by using Jan Tschichold's Sabon 14 point. He also arranged the text in phrases and separated them where the reader would naturally stop. Illustrated with sixty-six old masters paintings, Josef Albers also contributed art. It took over a decade to produce.

Many years later Angus Highland designed covers for The Pocket Canons, a series of small books featuring the text of individual books of the Bible drawn from the King James Version. Conceived by Matthew Darby, the series has sold over a million copies.

In 2007 the British design firm Crush produced a bible cover that shows the light and dark sides of biblical narrative through contemporary, appealing art. They say it is for "non-card-carrying Christians" and suggests a carnivalesque view of the Garden of Eden.

Although Darwin's theory may be questioned, the evolution of religious documents has taken many paths from the primordial to the present.

THE DESIGN OF NECROMANCY

MONUMENTS FOR THE DEAD GIVE RISE TO TYPOGRAPHIC IMMORTALITY.

In cemeteries rows and rows of stone markers carved with essentially the same basic image and letter styles are rooted in the traditions of consecrating the dead dating back centuries, even millennia. But this venerable practice has, of late, been brought into the twenty-first century through new technologies. A generational shift in customs has also influenced the way death is now being memorialized. With baby boomers approaching the twilight of "me" and "me-first" generations, death and its aftermath are more in the forefront, so new demands for personalized monuments are placed on both designers and manufacturers to break the classic molds.

Customizing memorials with personal graphics, including digital videos and expressive type-faces, mirror the quirks, eccentricities, and mythologies of the formerly sentient. However, this phenomenon is not altogether new. Take, for instance, the Egyptian pyramids or Grant's Tomb, just two examples of how the superego played a historical role in the design of necro-mancy. Now, thanks to new laser and digital technologies, you don't need to be a pharaoh or president to have an unprecedented monument or effigy—or, for that matter, a monumental effigy.

Stipulating in wills how, where, and by whom their monuments will be designed is increas-ingly more common, and they are not always the traditional monument makers. Before Paul Rand died in 1996, he asked (the now-late) Swiss designer Fred Troller to design a headstone that rejected timeworn clichés while serving the requisite function. The monument is com-posed of two heavy stone cubes, with the top one sitting ajar, carved with Rand's name and dates in sans-serif letters, evocative of the modernist sensibility Rand was so totally immersed in. Although surrounded in his Connecticut cemetery by traditional tombstones, his stands out for its economical beauty, subtle ingenuity, and elegant typography. What's more, a layer of polished stones is placed around the base because Rand did not want just any old rock left on the gravestone, as prescribed in Jewish tradition to indicate someone had visited the site.

An increased awareness of design in most areas of commercial life has been comparatively slow to impact the funeral industry; stones are routinely designed by monument companies or traditional letter-cutters. The latter is, however, a dying breed in the United States, although the apprentice system is still alive in Europe. Still, some designers have become involved in the field out of commitment to the need for change.

In 1996 the *New York Times* published a story about a New York architect, Ali Weiss, "turned tombstone designer" because she felt the American funeral industry depersonalized death. In an essay she wrote for *Tikkun* magazine she attacked the industry's "staggering lack of imagination" and "insensitivity to the demands of human spirit." She was appalled by the lack of aesthetics and abundance of commercialism. "I think baby boomers are going to take back control of the death-care industry," she told the *Times*, "the way they took back control of the childbirth experience—they are going to demand it be more meaningful." So she founded a company called "Living Monuments" and patented a process that features a five-hundred-word biography of the deceased in twenty-point type. The words are sandblasted onto a rotating component—oval, sphere, or rectangle—that is included as the integral part of the monument. Weiss's vision of the cemetery of the future is as a "library of past lives."

The trend to modernize gravestones using, among other things, images etched from photographs and artwork was covered in a 2005 *Boston Globe* story titled "Extreme Epitaphs." Comparing new approaches, reporter Douglas Belkin noted that "Tucked among the grim, gray headstones dating back 350 years in some New England cemeteries. . ." a new breed are being erected, ". . .some depict a bit of whimsy. Others, a touch of irreverence. All are deeply personal tributes to the deceased." But not everyone in the industry feels this is a positive development. The problem with personalized headstones, said Robert Fells, general counsel for the International Cemetery and Funeral Association in Virginia, is that "one person's dream is another person's nightmare." With computer technology any image

can be reproduced from any source, and some of those personal stones are adorned with Disney characters and Chevy trucks and all manner of typography, even the dreaded Comic Sans.

In 2004 a company called Vidstone began marketing "The Serenity Panel," a seven-foot solar-powered screen mounted on the front of a tombstone, which plays music and video about the deceased (they also market pet memorials). This high-tech version of the venerable enamel photograph of a late loved one has not, according to a 2007 CNN story titled "Death Goes Digital: The Electronic Tombstone," caught on yet. But it does note that more funeral homes are using LCD screens and multimedia tributes.

While monument and other funeral-industry companies are offering more variety than ever before, others argue that new trends in type and image design should still be governed by certain proprieties. Traditional serif faces are still the norm, but the computer has made the average consumer more familiar with various type "fonts" and so more likely to request novelty faces for their loved ones' monuments. So where is the line drawn? Historically, certain gravestones have been ostentatious, yet in the main shouldn't they still have an aura of solemnity? Can they veer too much from accepted norms? How do designers who work in this field mediate between old and new? Are there limits of taste?

I asked two tombstone designers to weigh in on how they practice their craft and what are their personal and imposed guidelines.

Ken Williams, a letter carver and design teacher from University of Georgia, Athens, began cutting letters out of his interest in history and maintains a sense of tradition in his work. "Letter artists/calligraphers are always wondering why is this hand/font shaped as it is—obviously its antecedent has a great deal to do with its form. And so you keep chasing things back into the past until you run into a wall (Hadrian's) or the Trajan column. For the Western World this is where it all started, form-wise." In the late '70s he found himself in southern Tuscany near a stone yard and a supplier where he bought chisels and tried to cut his own letters. After eight summers he had mastered the craft.

"There's not much call for cornerstones anymore," he said, "but as I got older more of my friends were dying and I started cutting their monuments."

Williams began his practice by replicating the classic Roman capital cut into stone from two thousand years ago. "It is almost impossible to beat. I will never master the nuances—you just keep noticing new things. I like to try to form the letters with a brush instead of copying a typeface. And I like to contrast the caps with the chancery hand. They are both elegant, one more formal, one more organic. Stone and hand-cut letters from the Roman or Renaissance periods seem magical."

One of his favorite projects is sun dials for two colleagues who had lost parents but wanted monuments in memorial gardens rather than cemeteries. They had shared times together in Italy and it seemed appropriate to use stones from that region and, because they were to be sited in a garden, to use parts of St. Francis's canticle extolling Mother Earth, Sister Moon, Brother Sun. (Unfortunately the canticle is shamelessly exploited for the tourist trade in Assisi). For the gnomon (the part of a sundial that casts the shadow), Williams had to figure out how to photo etch on both sides of a piece of brass. "If OSHA had only known what chemicals I was using in the university's darkrooms I would still be in jail," he said.

Williams notes that even in the arduous art of letter carving, he can do anything as long as the skill is there. But he has learned monument design is not a tabula rasa. He was once cutting in a stone shed in Elberton, Georgia (granite capital of the South) when a truck delivered a number of huge weathered pieces of stone cut in strange semicircles and triangles with sandblasted

lettering all over them. He asked the guys who worked there "What gives?" and they laughingly told him about the wacky doctor who designed his own monument, which looked like a spaceport for Martians. The doctor had died just a few days before; the widow called the stone shed to come and take down and haul away the embarrassing junk and cut the deceased a regular stone. "So I guess what you try not to do is make such an ungodly mess that the survivors won't rip it out of the ground."

Drew Dernavich is probably best known by *New Yorker* magazine readers for

his dryly witty cartoons signed with an upper- and lowercase, woodcut Dd. But for many years he has etched type and imagery into almost one thousand gravestones.

His uncle owned a company that imported granite into the United States from India, China, and Africa, and sold it to monument shops and retailers. Unlike the lighter granites from North America, these stones were dark and richly colored when polished, and they were looking for somebody who could etch portraits and realistic scenes onto them. "Because I was out of college and looking to apply my art skills somewhere, my uncle gave me the opportunity to try it out," recalls Dernavich, who adds that many if not most of the artists within the granite industry come from inside the industry itself.

He had done a fair amount of intaglio etching in college, so the approach of drawing white on black was familiar to him, although the specific tools were not. His tool of choice became the Dremel engraver, an electric tool that vibrates enough to carve a line into the surface of a stone, while still allowing for a lot of control. "It was the easiest thing to use and to travel with, although it took a long time for it to feel as comfortable as a pencil did in my hand."

Making imagery—the hand etching—used to be the only part of the stone carving process that was still done by hand. The stones are quarried and cut by machines, polished by machines, and carved and lettered by machines following programmed templates or rubber stencils. Dernavich notes there are probably more programmers in the business than stonecutters nowadays. And the etchings are following suit. Scanned images are etched by laser onto a stone very cheaply now. "The technology will undoubtedly change for the better, but these laser etchings tend to lack contrast and look flat and blurry, almost like a bad photocopy, except on a permanent piece of granite."

Dernavich worked for his uncle's company for a few years and also subcontracted with many other monument sellers in New England and New York, traveling to either their retail shops or manufacturer warehouses to do the work. By 1998 he had narrowed his clients down to six or seven dealers around Boston. "In many ways, this is an industry that's always at least a few years behind everybody else," he explains. "These businesses ran themselves without computers for years after they had become standard office equipment; one monument used rotary phones into the twenty-first century, and some shops don't even have bathrooms. The majority of the places I etch at look virtually the same as they did thirty years ago. I never regarded this as so much of a bad thing. When people shop for a monument they're less concerned with technological advancements, and more concerned with how well established the owners are—who they know in town, how familiar they are with the way things run, and how their fathers went to the same grade school together." The only time this tradition-bound industry frustrates him is when, as someone who works mostly outside of the gravestone industry, he believes he can bring a new image or design idea into a particular work. "Much of the time the answer I get is 'it's never been done that way,' with the assumption being that people aren't looking for something like that. It's a little better now, though, and it depends on the particular business owner."

But there are clear parameters. What can be put on a stone is limited by the rules of the individual cemetery, and tradition. Dernavich has etched logos of sports teams, album covers, cartoon characters, famous art works, restaurant facades, and beer insignias.

Gravestones have a long history of simplicity and ornamentation. A monument is one's last testament on Earth, and the last statement someone will ever make, so why not be as joyful or playful as possible?

Recently cemeteries have battled with families and monument shops over what could or couldn't be portrayed on a stone, predominantly in Catholic-owned cemeteries, where grave-lot owners were prohibited from featuring portraits or nonreligious scenery or phrases or imagery exceeding a certain size. Frequently a family would ask the shop to sneak an image by the gatekeepers. So, where portraits were prohibited, Dernavich etched an angel that just so happened to bear the exact likeness of the deceased, subscribing to the idea that who could say what an angel really looked like?

"There were several ridiculous instances of measuring, in inches, the size of an etched car or house or pet Yorkshire terrier, to make sure that it was not bigger than the crucifix in the middle of the stone, and all of the petty wrangling that would occur if a bishop decided that the stone looked too 'secular,'" he explains. "I can remember doing a landscape scene that partly depicted somebody's house and car, and having to integrate a giant glowing cross into it to offset the worldliness of the picture. There is also a sunset scene I did where I was instructed to do the same thing, because apparently sunsets on their own are not reverent enough." In terms of the subject matter, Dernavich does mostly portraits, followed closely by religious (mainly Catholic) imagery, and then, what he calls "stuff," meaning cars, trucks, motorcycles, boats, etc., with that category moving into the number two position eventually.

When it comes to drawing portraits, there is a disconnect between artist and subject. "The process of copying an 8 x 10 glossy photo is a no-brainer, and I always tell customers that if they give me a good picture I can make it look 'just like the person,' but we're seeing two different things. I'm seeing a photo of someone I never knew, and they're seeing an image loaded with love, grief, history, meaning, and context, and so there have been instances where I've captured an exact likeness (in my eyes), only to have a family tell me that it looks nothing like the person." Dernavich has, however, had a good track record, and out of the hundreds that he's done, only a few customers outright reject portraits, but when they have, it's because a family is too deep in grieving to be able to properly look at or communicate something, and it usually doesn't manifest itself until after the stone is finished.

New technologies and design attitudes may be apparent in more cemeteries today, but this is one craft where a greater widespread shift in typographic style and standards will be a hard rock to crack.

CAN DESIGN HELP THE USPS MAKE STAMPS POPULAR AGAIN?

THE POSTAL SERVICE'S NEW FOREVER STAMP SERIES, "SUMMER HARVEST," TARGETS TWO KINDS OF AUDIENCES: FOODIES AND NOSTALGICS.

In 1967, the United States Postal Service issued a new five-cent postage stamp to celebrate Henry David Thoreau's 150th birthday. The stamp proved exceedingly popular, but not for the reasons the USPS might have guessed: the scraggly-bearded portrait of Thoreau by Leonard Baskin became a generational emblem among members of the counterculture, who identified with Thoreau as a tax resister, abolitionist, and naturalist. The stamp's success, meanwhile, proved that nontraditional stamp designs could help the Postal Service connect with nontraditional audiences, especially among the nation's youth.

After 1971, when the USPS became an independent agency of the federal government, stamps became a vital revenue source. They were also the public face of the agency, and to broaden their appeal, the USPS and the Citizens Stamp Advisory Committee (CSAS) began to work on stamps that would attract not just philatelists but everyday shoppers. In a new attempt to engage a population that prefers email to snail mail, the USPS is hoping to continue this trend by selling stamps that reflect the sender's personal allegiances and resonate with their sensibilities.

Earlier this month, the agency issued a new booklet of produce-themed stamps titled "Summer Harvest." Designed and illustrated by the veteran illustrative letterer and typographer Michael Doret, who drew upon old fruit-and-vegetable-box labels for inspiration, the stamps seem to reflect the country's renewed interest in organic and locally sourced food.

Antonio Alcalá, the art director at CSAS, said the group had two main audiences in mind when designing the new Forever stamps: foodies and nostalgics. The stamps' decorative lettering and stylized images of watermelon, cantaloupe, sweet corn, and tomatoes seem aimed at the stereotypical modern yuppie, who listens to records on vinyl, visits the local farmer's market, shops for antiques, and might even occasionally forgo the ease of Gmail or Facebook in favor of writing and mailing a handwritten letter.

One of the challenges with producing stamps that capture a moment is that producing them is rarely a speedy process. The personnel on the committees change periodically, and the comments that come back from them are sometimes arcane. In the case of the "Summer Harvest" stamps, it took almost twelve years for them to get from the drawing board to the post office. "I went through literally dozens of changes on this recent set before we settled on the approved designs," says Doret. During the first round in 2002, he recalls there was a lot of back and forth suggesting various fruits or vegetables, then questioning what was the definition of "fruit," then questioning whether these were specifically "American." Even after his designs were accepted it still took about three years to get from refining the subject, artwork, and lettering to printing and issuance.

This isn't the first time the USPS has tried something new. In 1987, it commissioned the caricaturist Al Hirschfeld to design a collection of five stamps, called "Comedians by Hirschfeld," that were eventually released in 1991. Rather than the neutral portraiture typically used on commemorative stamps, his artwork introduced wit and humor to a serious and typically staid form. Hirschfeld became the first artist in American history to have his signature on a stamp booklet—not even Norman Rockwell had his name on the 1960 Boy Scouts stamp or the 1972 Tom Sawyer stamp he designed. The goofy personalities of the eight caricatured comedians (including Laurel & Hardy, Abbot & Costello, and Fanny Brice) elicited "chuckles from the letter-writing public," according to a 1991 article in the *New York Times*. By leaving its stuffy, disconnected traditions behind, the USPS had successfully tapped into the irreverent heart of pop culture.

Other recent Forever stamps have featured images of Elvis Presley, Maya Angelou, Batman, vintage roses, the Battle of 1812, and ferns. Last year, the "Farmers Market" series even celebrated American produce in the same way the "Summer Harvest" stamps do, although with a more traditional design. While the quality and variety of stamp designs has increased, 7.3 billion fewer pieces of mail are sent annually in the United States since "Comedians by Hirschfeld" revitalized the USPS's public image. The agency loses billions of dollars every year, and it's unlikely that a vintage-inspired set of stamps featuring crops can do much to change that, however visually striking they might be.

But the USPS's attempts to tap into the zeitgeist deserve credit, and the artists, designers, and art directors behind US postage stamps take extraordinary pride in creating them. "It's difficult to describe the thrill," says Doret, "of finding out that something into which one had invested so much time and love has now suddenly come back to life."

Michael Doret's 2015 Summer Harvest stamps are at once nostalgic and romantic visions of the contemporary farm-to-table ethos.

They not only celebrate natural food, the pencil-drawn sketch is natural art. *Courtesy Michael Doret.*

UNWRAPPED: THE SUBTLE JOYS OF FOOD PACKAGING

CELEBRATING THE ART OF WHAT OUR MEALS COME IN, FROM COOKIE BOXES TO CONDIMENT BOTTLES

In design jargon, "appetite appeal" describes the level of sensory stimulation that food packaging should have in order to attract consumers. A product covered with only type is by default less mouthwatering than one with photographs of a delicious chicken taco or cheese pizza.

But for brands, elegant typography and bold design can telegraph their own appetizing message. For more upscale chains like Trader Joe's and Whole Foods, getting customers to keep coming back is about more than just hunger: Food packaging has to signal reliability, trustworthiness, and consistency. Different companies might want to emphasize different qualities in their products—Trader Joe's, for example, might want to signal its quirky personality, while the New York–based minichain Fairway might emphasize value for money. But for every single product, design has to consider a wealth of different factors in order to best sell and market its products, and, on the whole, American stores are considerably less creative and inspired than their European counterparts.

First things first: shoppers aren't at the store for beautifully designed labels. They're there for food. So price is often the most important factor, particularly for staples such as milk, butter, eggs, and cereal. Other than a design snob, who really cares whether the Trader Joe's generic Bran Flakes box looks like the national brand, as long as the product is cheaper? And does it really matter that Fairway's "Golden Honey" plastic bear is a cloned copy of the more expensive original Dutch Gold Honey?

But good design is good business. Supermarket "private labels" don't have to be bland, and there are reasons, aside from aesthetic pleasure, why a little improvement can go a long way.

A package contains more than a product—it's a reliquary, of sorts, of that product's story (even its fabricated story), which can be a powerful selling tool. Scores of memorable brands have iconic packaging, like Heinz, Coca-Cola, and Kraft. Companies use bottles and labels to represent their respective reputations, which gives customers a certain pride of purchase and helps maintain the products' market superiority.

There's also a trend among certain independent brands to increase their footholds in competitive markets on the theory that a new product combined with striking design will be the tipping point. The unfettered, elegant packages for Siggi's yogurt, Sarabeth's jams, and Fizzie Lizzie beverages, if not iconic, have contributed to a pride of purchase among a growing number of loyal customers.

In 1998, I coauthored *Food Wrap,* a survey of new design styles and techniques for supermarket and specialty stores worldwide. The book's aim was to prove that food packaging was not entirely dictated by design conventions but by more fashionable and personal typography and illustration. In the late '80s, independent graphic-design studios were increasingly taking commissions away from traditional packaging design firms to create a new genre of premium products for a growing yuppie market. Then, during the '90s, a supermarket revolution of sorts took place, with stores undergoing modern redesigns and new upstart products becoming more visible in renovated aisles. Graphic designers found new ways to trigger consumers' Pavlovian responses through more nuanced typography, illustration, and color. The result was a dichotomy between mass-market and upscale products, with audiences often willing to pay more for food products that were designed with more sophistication.

While traditional supermarket brands are designed with straightforward imagery (a ripe tomato says tomato sauce) and stylized marquee logos, designs for the "fancy food" market are subtler in terms of logo, color, typography, and imagery. But in recent years, the line between the two sectors has blurred, with upscale design conceits being introduced to mainstream products.

No one does it better than the British chain Marks & Spencer on its Simply Food collection. Focusing on a young, middle-class, fashion-conscious audience, Charlotte Raphael-Graham, the store's head of graphic packaging, has created a culinary boutique of consistently beautiful and imaginative display-worthy packages featuring hundreds of products, from eggs to tea. The soothing colors, delightful illustrations, and vibrant typography, designed with wit, create a unified overall store identity and a pleasing shopping experience.

In a close second, the budget French chain Monoprix, has a range of colorful, carnivalesque packing designed by the French agency Havas City that busts supermarket conventions by using only bold sans-serif typefaces in caps covering all sides of the containers—not a picture of a sandwich or soup in sight. When all the products are displayed on the shelves, it's clear that a great design mind is at the helm. Havas has said that the aesthetic represents the "simplicity, humility, but also the cheerfulness of everyday life."

The same can't be said for Fairway. Its Magic Marker-esque Fairway logo doesn't complement other typefaces well, and most of its house brands seem like the name has been tacked on anywhere as an afterthought. Although nothing is egregiously ugly, there's a graphic dissonance

and brand disconnect between their specific products rather than an overarching direction, as though the supplier of each item made its own packaging, leaving an empty space for the Fairway logo.

The house design at Trader Joe's toes the line and sometimes achieves excellence. But here too, inconsistency reigns. Some of its cookie and cracker boxes, for instance, are given a nostalgic nineteenth-century engraving pastiche that suggests something from an old general store and implies "artisanal" production. But TJ's canned and frozen foods, including chili, garbanzo beans, and tomato sauce, retain the blandly generic supermarket look, customized only with the Trader Joe's logo. More attention to the overall graphic design may not influence all customers, but for those attuned to such things it can make all the difference between loyalty and not.

Only Whole Foods, which created a sophisticated yet simple "handcrafted" typographic style for its first store in Gowanus, Brooklyn, deliberately challenged all the rules of conventional supermarket packaging. Designed by Mucca in New York, the system is built solely on simple yet distinctive labels that are fixed to transparent bags and plastic containers. Rather than use a photograph, the actual product—whether seven-grain bread, guacamole, or linguini—is its own illustration. And what further sets the packages apart from other premium products is how well they are integrated into a larger design system throughout the store. The entire environment exudes appetite appeal.

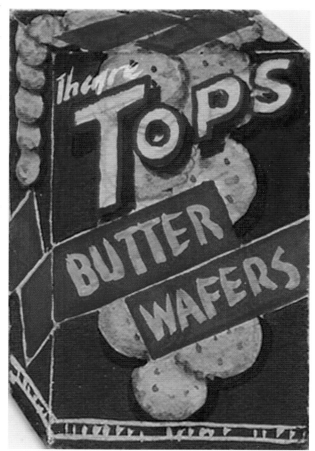

Critics of packaging argue that the best package is no package, suggesting a return to the venerable ways of selling food in bulk from burlap bags and wooden barrels. But branded packaged goods are not going away just yet, and good design can not only addresses sustainability issues, but also make the stressful supermarket experience a little more enjoyable.

These are by no means contemporary food packages. Nor are they retro designs for future nostalgic brands. But they are handpainted (c.1948) studies for packages that might have been. *Courtesy Jim Heimann.*

GRAPHIC DESIGN AS VISUAL DIALECT

GRAPHIC DESIGN AS VISUAL DIALECT

—

LETTERS AND TYPEFACES, SIGNS AND SYMBOLS ARE VISUAL REPRESENTATIONS OF VERBAL LANGUAGE. THEY MAKE SOUNDS AND EXUDE EMOTION; THEY TRIGGER PERSONAL RESPONSES IN READERS. FOR DESIGNERS, TYPE IS A TOOL AND A FETISHISTIC OBJECT. TYPE RESONATES BEYOND THE OBVIOUS. HERE, WE SEE TYPE PILFERING IS EXAMINED AS BOTH AN INTELLECTUAL PROPERTY INFRACTION AND A PERSONAL VIOLATION. TYPEFACE NAMES OFTEN EXEMPLIFY THE VALUES IMBUED IN TYPE BY THEIR DESIGNERS. AND LETTERS THEMSELVES ARE CHARGED WITH MEANING AS SIGNIFICANT AS ANY PIECE OF ART. TYPE, IMAGERY, AND LETTERS SPEAK JUST AS LOUDLY AS THE VOICE.

YOU WOULDN'T THINK IT, BUT TYPEFACE PIRACY IS A BIG PROBLEM

MOST PEOPLE HAVE NO IDEA THAT FONTS, LIKE MUSIC OR MOVIES, ARE PROTECTED BY INTELLECTUAL PROPERTY LAWS.

It's safe to assume that most people have no idea that fonts, like music or movies, are protected by intellectual property laws, they usually come with a hefty price tag, and they are uncommonly vulnerable to unjust adaptation and outright theft.

This makes sense if you think about it. Type always has been a popular commodity, and its profusion across our digital devices has only boosted demand. Typefaces are of monumental importance in the mobile era, essential both as a means of clearly communicating information and distinguishing one app or website from another. Even people beyond the design world have grown familiar with the stylistic differences of type design, and increasingly selective about the fonts they use. Fluency, appreciation, and preference have conspired to turn type design into a lucrative business.

It is hard to say if rates of plagiarism and outright piracy have increased, but this much is clear: In an era when files can be shared with the click of a mouse and anyone with a computer is an ersatz typographer, copyright infringement has never been easier to commit. The laws protecting type are weak at best, but designers are fighting back with lawsuits and purchasing models aimed at dissuading theft and converting would-be pirates into customers.

What Makes a Font?

There are tens of thousands of typefaces, ranging from the Times New Roman and Calibri found in every word-processing program to more specialized fonts like Apple's San Francisco and our own font, Exchange. Designing typefaces used to involve working with wood and metal to create movable type. These days, the process is largely digital. That doesn't mean designing and manufacturing a new typeface is any less challenging. Specialized software called font editors help streamline the creative process, but designing a typeface from the ground up remains a difficult and time-consuming affair.

Consider the work of Jonathan Hoefler, founder of type foundry H&Co. Whether working from a sixteenth-century printing type—like the one that inspired Quarto—or the style of sign-making that gave rise to Gotham, the primary typeface of Obama's presidential campaigns, Hoefler and his team never create a "new" font by directly modifying an old one. Instead, says Hoefler, "We explore the ideas behind a collection of physical artifacts, and interpret them as a family of digital fonts." In other words: When H&Co turns to a historical typeface for inspiration, its designers don't just redraw it. Where an uninspired type designer might trace an old font and add a serif, Hoefler's team will deconstruct a reference typeface, study the elements that make its letterforms unique from an aesthetic or structural standpoint, then reassemble it in a unique way.

That's not to say type designers don't model new fonts after old designs. These are what are called "revivals." Frank Martinez, a New York intellectual property lawyer specializing in type design cases, says the primarily rationale behind a revival "is usually to create a digital version of an otherwise unavailable typeface." This is often necessary, because older typefaces tend to harbor quirks that arose from the mechanical constraints under which they were created. Nuances in form that were acceptable when printing on a letterpress, for example, might appear sloppy on a crisp, high-definition display. Even modern, digital typefaces often can be improved or expanded upon, says Dan Rhatigan, freelance type designer and former art director at Monotype. "In short, if we base a new product on an older design, it's because that design wasn't enough, in some way," he says.

James Montalbano, the Brooklyn-based founder of Terminal Design, compares his trade to the fashion business. "Every designer should have their version of the little black dress, the three-piece suit, formal wear, casuals, et cetera," he says. "Type design is no different—there are basic historical genres that underpin all type design."

That's the thing about type design: like all artistic endeavors, it always has relied on derivation—but ingenuity is essential, too. "There's a lot of room for originality, on many levels," says Hoefler, and that originality requires a major investment on the part of the designer. Creating Quarto, despite having access to plenty of source material, took nine years. "Compare the process behind a project like Quarto," he says, "with the act of generating a typeface by beginning with someone else's fully realized font."

When you understand what goes into creating a typeface, it becomes clear why type foundries charge for their designs. Today, digital font packages are commonly licensed for web use, or for installation on one or more computers. Prices vary considerably, depending on the typeface and foundry in question. A company might charge ninety-nine dollars for permission to use a specific typeface on the web, or one thousand dollars to install a font on, say, twenty computers. But commissioning a brand-new, custom typeface can cost upwards of fifty thousand dollars per face.

It's also easy to see how piracy or plagiarism could be tempting. Making a font is hard. Stealing a font, or tweaking an existing font and calling it your own, is much easier.

It's Easy Being a Pirate

Plagiarism and theft are easy because the United States doesn't have specific, quantitative definitions or standards dictating just how much a typeface must be altered before it qualifies as a "new" font. Similarly, there are no copyright laws protecting the design of any given letter, style, shape, or brushstroke. Oh sure, there are some firm rules: you can't use a trademarked name like Quarto to describe your ripped-off font, and you can't use the same code or software as the original designer. But these are small hurdles to a determined copycat. "If a design is perceived as successful," Montalbano says, "someone will attempt a knockoff."

Piracy is even easier to commit. Never mind hackers—designers have been known to steal fonts from their own companies' libraries. Online, freely accessible font archives like DaFont regularly list knockoff versions of original designs under modified names; while sites like The Pirate Bay provide easy access to massive typeface collections—some with upwards of sixty-five thousand fonts.

It wasn't always this easy. Digital type piracy started slowly in the 1980s, around the time fonts began making the leap to computers. But things picked up in the early 1990s with the transition to the modern Internet. In 1998, the Digital Millennium Copyright Act made it easier for type foundries to issue takedown notices to freeloading websites. Those who refused, says Carima El-Behairy, cofounder of P22 Type Foundry and a veteran of piracy wars, "became liable of hosting illegal software." Such policing soon became Sisyphean, though.

Lawsuits are another option, though information surrounding copyright infringement cases is usually hard to come by. Most designers interviewed for this story, for example, declined to name those they had sued or the penalties agreed upon, citing confidentiality clauses in their settlements. But every once in awhile, one of these cases pops up in the news.

To Catch a Pirate

In 2009, The Font Bureau, one of America's leading type foundries, sued NBC Universal for failing to secure the rights to a handful of its trademarked fonts—fonts the media giant had used to promote programs like *The Tonight Show* and *Saturday Night Live.*

According to the Society of Publication Designers, Font Bureau argued that NBC paid for just a single license—which permitted the company to install the typefaces on a single computer—and the rights to a limited number of fonts. "But NBC went ahead and copied the fonts to a bunch of other computers within the company," SPD reported, "and also started using several other fonts for which licenses were never obtained."

It was a big case. Font Bureau asked for "no less than $2 million" in damages. It argued that NBC's unauthorized use "caused injury to Font Bureau's relationships with present and prospective customers" and would "cause confusion, mistake, and deception as to the source of Font Bureau's trademarks," making it more difficult to broker licensing deals with other companies. The case was settled out of court, as nearly all such cases are.

A similar scenario played out in 2012, when designers working on a campaign website for presidential hopeful Rick Santorum allegedly used a typeface called Fedra without paying for it. Peter Bil'ak—the founder of Dutch type foundry Typotheque and Fedra's creator—accused Raise Digital of using an "unauthorized derivative version" of the trademarked font on Santorum's site. Not only had they modified it ever so slightly, Bil'ak said the firm wasn't licensed to use Fedra on the site. Bil'ak hired IP lawyer Frank Martinez, who argued that Raise Digital had deprived Typotheque of $2 million in fees.

The site ultimately was shuttered, and the lawyers worked out a no-cure-no-pay agreement. Raise Digital paid some legal fees, too. "But it was peanuts," says Bil'ak.

Solutions

Of course, campaign website designers and media companies aren't the only ones stealing fonts. Montalbano says many of them are "hobby/collector" or DIYers, whose decision to pick and choose from font-sharing websites presupposes a social license to access all web assets for personal use. "I do think that there is an 'everything on the internet should be free' attitude," he says.

El-Behairy, of P22 Type Foundry, believes there's another psychological factor at play. "I think it is laziness," she says. "Why should [users] license the original if it is available for free? There is a prevailing attitude that fonts do not have the value of other software, so why should they pay for it?"

She believes font-sharing sites should suffer stiffer penalties when they're caught with pirated software, but Bil'ak takes a more pragmatic view. Laws, he says, cannot change human nature, so the onus is on designers to rethink how fonts are licensed. "The only way to fight the piracy is to make alternative products more accessible and affordable," he says. He's described his company, Fontstand, as "the iTunes of fonts." The goal, he says, is to allow users to try fonts for free, or rent them on a monthly basis.

Meanwhile, Rudy VanderLans, cofounder of Emigre Fonts and a dogged opponent of copyright infringement, admonishes students and businesses alike: "Don't steal from others. I know it's not that simple, but if you absolutely have to 'appropriate' the work of others, and you're in doubt whether it's legal, ask for permission. You'd be surprised how easy that is, and how it can be mutually beneficial." Like Bil'ak, VanderLans says he would rather find reasonable ways to make his fonts available through short-term rentals and other means than endure the costly consequences of piracy. Many would-be infringers, he believes, are future customers in disguise.

"Greed plays a smaller part than ever before," says Rhatigan. "It's usually a case of ignorance about licensing and copyright, or laziness about how to go about exploring a twist on an existing design," he says. "Overzealous thrift is probably more to blame now that it is so easy to copy digital data, and so temptingly easy to just open up a file and begin tinkering with it to make it something else." That's the double-edged sword of digital magic—what is old can be manipulated to become something either amazingly new or dubiously borrowed. The line between those two can be vanishingly small.

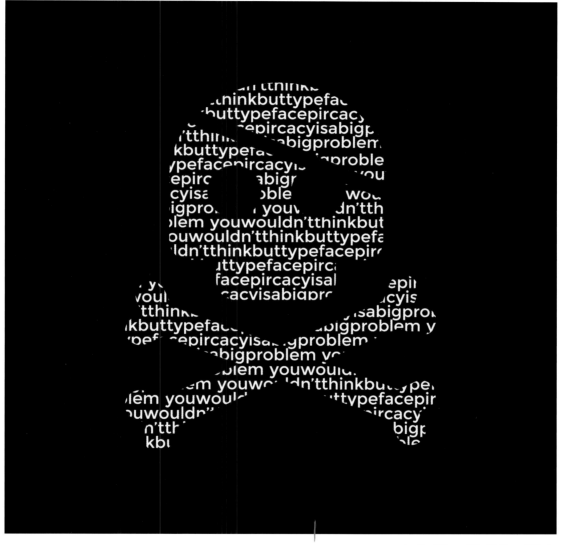

Anaële Pélisson/The Collected Works

TYPEFACES BY ANY OTHER NAMES

SOME TYPEFACE NAMES ARE SILLY, OTHERS ARE UNFORGETTABLE, MANY ARE INCONSEQUENTIAL.

When the time comes for soon-to-be parents to name their newborns, there are plenty of books and websites to help find the fashionable or distinctive moniker. A typeface is a type designer's baby, yet there is zilch on what to name it after all those months of labor. If a guidebook were available, it might offer the same wisdom as this paraphrase from the précis to a popular infant naming site:

There's a lot of pressure in choosing a font name. It'll be one of the first things people learn about your typeface and will be a part of its life. Though naming your new face is a daunting process, it can also be fun. Some designers discuss and research—and argue about the name until it is released. Other designers just hear a name and love the sound. There are about as many ways to pick a name as there are names themselves.

Even if naming a font is not actually that difficult, the result is consequential. It shouldn't be too loony or obscure or uptight. One of the more conventional options is to name it after a living or dead family member or friend or a real-life or fictional person. Or to play it safe, while insuring a modicum of immortality, it might just be as simple to use the designer's name—it is done all the time.

The following names are memorable—Robert Granjon, Philippe Grandjean de Fouchy, John Baskerville, Claude Garamond, Pierre Simon Fournier, Aldus Manutius, Nicolas Jensen, and of course Giambattista Bodoni—because revivals of the original types that they designed or punch-cut bear their surnames. And by virtue of these names being so prominent, their brands live on from one iteration to the next and one generation to the next.

If these same fonts were anonymously conceived, they could have been forgotten long ago. But a name provides pedigree, like a signature on a painting. History remembers those who are known. A famous name makes a famous typeface or vice versa.

Lending proper names to fonts did not all of a sudden happen. "In Bodoni's *Manuale Tipgrafico* of 1818, over one hundred romans and italics are shown with the name of a city as a kind of nickname," Tobias Frere-Jones explained on his blog (October 9, 2014), "though the real name was still a size and a number." Trieste is really Ascendonica (22 point) No. 9, Palermo is Sopracanoncino (28 point) No. 3, et cetera, et cetera. It may not have occurred to Bodoni to call a face by his own name, so it was left to others much later after his death. By the mid-nineteenth century, typefaces were given descriptive names and numbers, or what Frere-Jones called "a tally" of attributes with names like Gothic Condensed No. 7 or Paragon Italian Shaded. Many fonts were only numbered with a catalog reference.

The rise of industry and consumers in the early to mid-nineteenth century necessitated the invention of advertising, which required unique eye-catching typefaces as hooks for consumers. To meet the demand, foundries created decorative, ornamented, and what later were called novelty types and were given names that either celebrated something or someone, or reflected their respective styles. For instance, Rustic (1845) was an alphabet made of logs (aka Log Cabin) at the Vincent Figgins Foundry.

Floride is not named in honor of toothcare, but like many names it is memorable because it is so unique and seemingly random.

It is not known which typeface was the first to be named for the designer, but by the late nineteenth century, foundries found it commercially prudent to exploit the relative fame of their most respected designers. Frederic Goudy's Goudy Oldstyle and Goudytype originally named by ATF became models for eponymous self-promotion of Goudy's Village Press & Letter Foundery. Other designers in Europe and the United States understood the marketing value of linkage with reputation: Otto Eckmann's Eckmannschrift; Eric Gill's Gill Sans; Louis Oppenheim's LO-Type; Lucian Bernhard's Bernhard Gothics, Brushscripts, and a Roman called Lucian; Marcel Jacno's Jacno; and so many more. Later, Ed Benguiat's ITC Benguiat and ITC Benguiat Gothic were emblematic of the 1970s. And while Herb Lubalin's Avant Garde was his bestselling collaborative font, he only gave his name to ITC Lubalin Graph. Many type designers, however, were reluctant to capitalize on their own fame in this way. W. A. Dwiggins and Stanley Morrison immediately come to mind.

What to name a typeface is still a difficult decision, but eponymous typefaces are less frequent today than earlier in the twentieth century. End of the me-generation, perhaps? Naming is more similar to rock bands, like Geogrotesque and Brunswick Black. Or imbued with psychological and personal associations, like Eric Gill's Joanna or Daniel Pelavin's Anna, both named for their daughters. Or a name can reference the source material on which the face was conceived, like Frere-Jones' Interstate, based on specifications for highway signage. In the final analysis, perhaps a typeface name is not like any other name because, well, it sounds good.

THE MANY MEANINGS OF K

LET ME COUNT THE KS.

In the alphabetic hierarchy *A* gets all the attention and *Z* comes in last, but the most symbolically crafty of all the letters is *K*. Although sometimes known as soft and silent, when hard it is the strongest of the twenty-six, not just in English but in German too. The look, sound, and weight of *K* are so keenly experienced yet often overlooked, it's time to pronounce this K-day and kindle a kind of celebration for the kingpin of stand-alone letters.

There are so many ways people have capitalized on *K*:

Henry Chadwick, creator of the venerable baseball box score, chose K to symbolize a strikeout because it was the last letter in struck as in "struck out." It has stuck like tar for over a hundred years.

In Franz Kalfka's *The Trial*, Josef K is arrested by two unidentified agents from an unspecified agency for an unspecified crime. The agents' boss later conducts a minitribunal in the room of K's neighbor, Fräulein Bürstner. K is not taken away, however, but left free and told to await instructions from the Committee of Affairs.

K-rations were invented by Dr. Ancel Keys (from which the K derives) in 1941. The government assigned him to design a nonperishable, ready-to-eat meal that could fit in a soldier's pocket as a short-duration, individual ration. Keys choose supermarket foods that would be inexpensive and provide energy. "The meals only gained 'palatable' and 'better than nothing' ratings from the soldiers, but were successful in relieving hunger and providing sufficient energy."

Special K, the rice and wheat cereal, was introduced in 1955 four years after Kellogg Company's founder, W. K. Kellogg, died at the age of ninety-one. His body lay in state for three days in the main lobby of the company office building so that hundreds of workers and Battle Creek residents could pay their respects—now that was special.

K2 is the world's second-highest peak (28,251 feet) second only to Everest; it is located in the Karakoram Range in a Chinese-administered part of Kashmir within the Uygur Autonomous Region of Xinjiang, China.

K2 is also a new type of synthetic marijuana, known as Spice. It is known to cause illness and can be fatal in certain doses.

K4s are very small, yellow, easily crushed pills that contain 4 milligrams of hydromorphone under the brand name Dilaudid. They contain no harmful filler ingredients and are safe to inject directly into the veins. Kicks are getting harder to find.

K9 is the military designation for a dog, the transliteration of the word canine.

K in science literature is an abbreviation of kalium, the Latin name for potassium.

K is a unit of measure for temperature based upon an absolute scale.

K is short for *kilo*.

K is used to refer to numbers or distance in thousands, 1k = 1,000.

K signifies the color black of K for key—a shorthand for the printing term key plate, printing in black ink as in CYMK.

K-particle or kaon, also called a K meson, and shortened to K has something to do with quarks (or quacks).

K for *kindergarten* was a term coined by Friedrich Fröbel, a visionary German educator, whose approach influenced early-years education. The raging issue today is equal pre-K opportunities.

K in German, as in the spelling of America as "Amerika" (and the title of another Kafka novel) has been used to compare the United States to European dictatorships.

K is also shorthand for OK, which is given many origins, among them as an abbreviation of "orl korrekt," a jokey misspelling of "all correct" which was current in the United States in the 1830s.

KKK is among the most hateful of the many usages—Kooks, Killers, Klan—and not necessary to celebrate here.

If you have more K usages, applications, abbreviations, words, or stories, send them to us. . . . K?

K. Sculpture © June Corley.

MARKING INDECENCY

A LOOK AT THE SULTRY HISTORY OF THE XXX SIGN AND THE UBIQUITOUS USE OF THE LETTER X

X is the sexiest letter in the alphabet—think of two people and four legs intertwined—and certainly one of the most symbolically diverse. X is the sign of the kiss in xoxo (kisses and hugs). It is Roman numeral 10. It substitutes for a signature (as in make your X). It locates treasure on a map (X marks the spot). It factors into mathematical equations (a + b = x). It is a signifier for extra strength. It is short for excision. It is prefix for the sound barrier–breaking experimental aircraft the X-15. It represents the number of strikes in both baseball and bowling. It substitutes for Christmas (Xmas). A former partner is an "ex." A long time ago, when they were scrawled on beer kegs, Xs indicated the amount of tax paid by tavern owners—and of course, speaking of beer, Dos Equis comes to mind. And let's not forget Malcolm X—the X repudiated and excised the last name of the white slave-masters who brutalized his ancestors.

Whatever its meaning or significance, people understand X has import and, given the context, they seem to know what each X means.

The most recognized X is the one used for the MPAA film rating system. This letter sign, which prohibits "persons under eighteen" from admittance to any film featuring graphic sexual or violent content, began in the United States in 1968, replacing the censorious Hays Code. However, X was part of the UK's Board of Film Classification, starting in 1951 (replacing an H for Horror). This X rating stopped persons younger than sixteen from being admitted into dicey films; it was later replaced by R18 (Restricted 18), which exed out the X altogether.

X is a stop sign that beckons. X is the promise of danger, rebellion, even subversion. Add two more Xs and the symbolic and cognitive stakes are exponentially raised. XXX is taboo, extra strength, out of the norm, extremely potent—it is raw sex. A storefront with the triple X brand is less than wholesome. XXX is the quintessence of seedy.

Like most things vernacular, it evolved gradually and circuitously. X became sexualized in the 1960s when the film industry realized that an X rating both limited the range of distribution

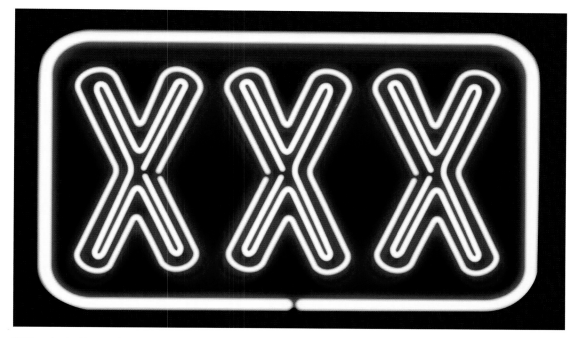

XXX marks the G-spot. *Courtesy* Print *magazine.*

and extended the opportunities to sell through alternative outlets. X means bad, which makes it good in certain quarters. In the late 1960s, pornography was becoming tolerated and as a result, it become more chic. X-rated films were in great demand and the unholy X (whether bestowed by the MPAA or not) was a sales aid—signaling that graphic sex was in generous supply (today's HBO series would have gotten X [or later NC-17] ratings). Eventually, film distributors needed radical distinctions between the tame X, which involved full-frontal nudity, XX, which suggested simulation of the sex act, and XXX, which flaunted hardcore sex.

The X was never officially codified by a governing body, but the definition of XXX is universally acknowledged as breaking the ceiling of bad.

MORE THAN A COLOR

WHAT DO YOU SEE WHEN YOU SEE RED? THE ASSOCIATIONS ARE MANY.

When anger turns to fury, do you see red?

Probably not.

"Seeing red" is merely a metaphor. It vividly describes rage, but unless you are predisposed to rosacea, a skin condition in which the blood vessels dilate, ocular chromatic changes are not triggered even by as intense a human emotion as anger. "Seeing red" is just clever wordplay that colors the way we think of anger.

Red is a powerful modifier.

Is it possible to be caught literally red-handed? Maybe, if you were stealing from farmer McGregor's strawberry patch, but otherwise guilt does not physically alter hand color. Nonetheless this literal figure of speech refers back to a time when being discovered with blood on one's hands after committing a violent criminal act was a sure sign of guilt. Few colors can be more vivid than blood red.

Red has more literal references than any other color and greater symbolic power—good and bad—than any other hue, including black. Just consider some of the most common associations—blood, death, revolution, love, sex, envy, heat, and fire. "Red hot" is the most intense of heats. "Redneck" is the lowest of social classes. "Red flag" is the anticipation of trouble. Rudolf the "Red-Nosed" Reindeer is first among reindeers. Then there is the red-light district, The Woman in Red, Little Red Riding Hood, Red Devil, and red state. To redline suggests racial profiling and discrimination while a red cross is symbolic of emergency medical service. The red shield of the Salvation Army represents "the blood which was shed by Jesus for our sins." Red signs are the most visible and powerful on road or street. Red pencil means deletion, while a red-letter day, derived from medieval times when church calendars announced holy days in red, means today is a special occasion. My son went to the "Little Red Schoolhouse" for lower and middle school—red schools came into par-

lance after log buildings were phased out and sawed weatherboard siding was painted red for protection from the elements.

Red is a volatile color. Giuseppe Garibaldi, who famously fought for Italian independence from Napoleonic rule in the nineteenth century, had all his fighters dress in the *camicia rossa*. They were called "Redshirts"—the living signs of rebellion and unification. On a more sinister note: "We chose red for our posters, since it is vivid and was the color that most aroused our opponents. It forced them to notice and remember us," Adolf Hitler wrote in his memoir *Mein Kampf.* He borrowed the color from the Soviet Flag or "red banner," which paid homage to the red flag of the 1871 Paris Commune. The communist red flag represents the blood shed in the war for emancipation from the Russian Czar. Red has long been a positive Russian color, with the Russian word for red, *krasny,* related to the word for beautiful, *krasivyy.* In China red symbolizes good fortune and joy and is found on banners and posters galore. George Washington is thought to have taken red for the American flag from the British colors (Red Coats), but the white stripes signified the secession from the home country.

Red is a joyful color. "I love red so much that I almost want to paint everything red," Alexander Calder said. Frank Lloyd Wright used red as the color of the square signature tile that was placed on his houses during the 1930s. "Where I got the color red—to be sure, I just don't know," Henri Matisse once remarked about his beautiful painting *The Red Studio.* "I find that all these things . . . only become what they are to me when I see them together with the color red." Pablo Picasso, however, famously said, "If I don't have red, I use blue."

Red is a dominant color. Most artists and designers are not as cavalier about red as Picasso was. The primary Bauhaus colors were red, yellow, and blue, but red was the most iconic—along with black. ReD (*Revue Devětsilu* 1927 to 1931) was the title of the Czech avant-garde magazine

Shades of red.

The reds of modernism: *De Reclame* on avant garde advertising.

Typographische Mitteilungen is Jan Tschichold's praise of red and black.

edited by Karel Tiege, which often used red ink for its mnemonics and visibility. And El Lissitzky famously "Beat the Whites With the Red Wedge."

Red is a dangerous color. Think Red Alert or Code Red. It is a cautionary color warning against threatened danger. The universal STOP sign need not have any type on it as long as red fills its octagonal shape. The bold letters of a "Wrong Way" dropped out of red are as powerful a message as a sign can telegraph. But not all red signs have safety as their goal. The red and black of neo-Nazi banners harkens back to the Fascist era when red and evil were synonymous. But red is not owned by one group alone. Thailand's 2010 antimilitary junta protesters belonging to The National United Front of Democracy Against Dictatorship were issued red shirts (and called Red Shirts too) as a sign of solidarity.

Not all red is created equal. Josef Albers noted, "If one says 'red' and there are fifty people listening, it can be expected that there will be fifty reds in their minds. And one can be sure that all these reds will be very different." There are many different kinds: imperial red, ruby red, rusty red, fire engine red, barn red, or crimson. Lipstick red comes in even more alluring shades. Was the Scarlet Letter any of these, or its own shade of persecution? Incidentally, red hair is really orange. Red wine is made from dark-colored grapes.

Every color has applied significance invented by man but given mystical and psychological significance. The package design website "empower-yourself-with-color-psychology" interprets red this way:

"Red means energy, action, passion, excitement and strength.

"Dark reds are perceived as professional and luxurious, while bright reds are more exciting and energetic and generally of lower perceived value than dark reds.

Red speaks: article in *De Reclame* on the power of red and in *American Printer* a revue of red in everyday printing.

"Blue-reds are more attractive to the upper class market, while orange-reds are attractive to the working class—orange-reds have a lower perceived price and value.

"But adding black decoration to your red packaging can add sexual or adult connotations."

Red is a color about which everyone has an opinion. Red is good. Red is bad. Red is power. Red is love. Red is warmth. Red is evil. Red is Santa. Red is the Devil. This should make red the most confusing color on the spectrum. If everyone sees red differently, then what is the real red? The answer is both universal and individual. But next time you order red, think first about all the implications; the wrong use may turn your face red with embarrassment.

The Soviet flag: red as symbol of revolution.

Gustav Klustis's Worker Men and Women: Everyone Vote in the Soviet Elections, 1930.

MORE THAN AN ALBUM COVER

PAULA SCHER'S BOSTON COVER WAS NOT HER FAVORITE, BUT MANY LOVE IT DEARLY.

Boston's hit song "More Than a Feeling" has long been a frequent presence on movie soundtracks and at wedding receptions. Just as instantly recognizable, though, is the cover of the eponymous first album on which the song appears. Designed by Paula Scher and illustrated by Roger Huyssen for Epic Records, the cover has a loyal following equaling the iconic art for The Beatles' *Revolver* (designed by Klaus Voorman) and Cream's *Disraeli Gears* (Martin Sharp). Album covers often carry emotive and symbolic weight—but what is it about guitar-shaped spaceships fleeing an exploding planet Earth on Boston that makes the image so special?

Scher, who once designed covers and worked as an art director for major artists such as The Rolling Stones and Maynard Ferguson, admits she's "mystified" by the continued interest in this album package. "The Boston cover was designed in 1976 and is now thirty-nine years old," she says. "It was, and still is, in my opinion, a mediocre piece of work."

Yet the album has endured: the guitar-ship has been repeated on subsequent records and as backdrops on concert stages.

Album images don't always turn out as planned—their popularity is often a matter of timing. Take the cover for *Boston*: Tom Scholz, the band's guitarist and songwriter, wanted a guitar on the cover, which in Scher's artistic lexicon was a cliché. She and Epic Records product manager Jim Charney compromised with a guitar-shaped spaceship. "The first spaceship cover idea we showed Scholz had a Boston invasion of the planet, but Scholz said that spaceships should be saving the planet, not attacking. So we came up with the Earth-blowing-up idea," she said.

The cover would have become iconic anyway, says Lenny Kaye, the guitarist, author, and Patti Smith collaborator, since the album was an out-of-box success. Yet the cover art "gave it a science-fictional feel, as if Martians had landed and took over Earth using a particularly post-apocalyptic guitar tone and frequency."

To rockers at the time, the ambiguity of the design worked in its favor. "There was something special and risky about albums that did not show the band," said Joe Butler, the drummer for The Lovin' Spoonful. "It allowed you to imagine what and who was behind the music." Kaye concurred. "Surely one could read just about anything into it," he said. "And its color scheme of many warm colors certainly enhanced the lighting of the bong."

But does the image have more resonance than the band and the song it accompanied? The cultural significance of the art for *Boston* lives on: Just last year on NPR's *Wait, Wait, Don't Tell Me*, when host Peter Sagal did a bit about the Earth blowing up and spaceships leaving the planet, he made the connection: "You know, like the *Boston* cover."

Three other Boston albums, all with similar spaceships, have been produced since that first one—all with strong designs by real science illustrators. "But no one talks about *them*," Scher says. "They only talk about this one, and continually! It is a total vernacular item. Everyone knows what it looks like."

Paula Scher's 1976 least favorite indelible record cover.

CUTE AS A BUG

FROM BABY ANIMALS TO MASCOTS, WHY CAN'T WE GET ENOUGH OF "CUTE"?

The adult trilobite, an extinct marine arthropod that flourished during the Paleozoic era, isn't—and will never be—cute. Its spiky, furrowed exoskeleton is otherworldly and "butt-ugly." But squint hard enough and the baby trilobite could be cute. Virtually any living thing in its infant state, even a cockroach, has appeal by virtue of its diminutive features. Smallness hides many sins. Yet not all things infantile are *a priori*, Shirley Temple–precious or Olsen twins–sweet. The baby Jesus isn't cute; he's mystical. But the baby in *Look Who's Talking* is, or was (a cute baby doesn't guarantee a cute adult).

The word in question derives from *acute*. At some point in the nineteenth century, it became slang for certain kinds of alluring traits and became synonymous with adorable-in-the-extreme. Routinely applied to humans and animals (although baby vegetables are kind of cute too), extreme cuteness often triggers the involuntary yearning to hug in an aggressive way. For example, bunnies, piglets, and puppies are so delectably cute we could "just eat them up." Likewise, parrots and parakeets dressed in pirate outfits are both cute and funny. Cute is irresistible. Lennie Small, the dim-witted character in John Steinbeck's *Of Mice and Men*, stroked a puppy so hard he unknowingly squeezed the life out of it. Although extreme, it represents the inexplicable sensation many of us have to devour cuteness—to become one with it.

Cuteness is a powerful tool in the visual manipulator's toolkit, right up there with sex. There are a couple of variations, though: basic cute (i.e., oozing with sweetness) and excessively cute (i.e., Shirley Temple in *Glad Rags to Riches*). Basic cute evokes the urge to hold the cute thing for hours, while excessive (or radical) cute demands stimulation beyond the point of logic, triggering the aforementioned uncontrollable, overpowering desire to squeeze, snuggle, and hug. I'm not going to examine the psychological phenomena or the philosophical constructs of cute, though; rather, I'm concerned with how cute imagery has evolved from the twentieth to twenty-first century.

In 1949, zoologist Konrad Lorenz codified "cute," observing that the typical baby face—big eyes, large head in comparison to small body and nose—melts the heart in a maternal or paternal way.

This is true for living creatures and inanimate objects, including dolls and stuffed animals. The most famous cutie doll is the Kewpie Doll, a cherubic, cupid-inspired fairy conceived in 1912 as a cartoon character by Rose O'Neill, and later turned into a mass-market figurine. With its bulbous head, puffy cheeks, big bright eyes, and rotund little belly, this baby doll took the nation by storm.

The Inuit are a native people, not animal mascots.

Many commercial-product mascots score high on the cute quotient, one of the most effective and enduring being the Pillsbury Doughboy. Created by Martin Nodell's team at Leo Burnett in 1965, the Doughboy's chubby, squishy marshmallow body has all the tactility of freshly rolled dough and the physique of a freshly delivered baby. In his commercials, when his belly is lovingly poked or tickled, he lets out an ecstatic little chuckle, and you "just want to eat him up" (or squash him, depending on your mood).

In 1983, the Snuggle Bear puppet for Snuggle fabric softener was developed by Kermit Love, and when it's animated, the adorable bear embodies the same poppin' fresh attributes as the Doughboy. Both rely heavily on matching the cutest features to the cutest voice. Whoever thought of the Charmin Bears (named Molly, Leonard, Bill, Amy, and Dylan, for the record) understood that cute adds wit to the bodily function conversation. In one recent commercial, a piece of toilet paper sticks to a bear's butt—one of the larger complaints about toilet tissue—to get to the message that Charmin is stickfree. The Android's mascot, a robot designed by Irina Blok, is known as the "bugdroid," and shows that nonhuman or animal characters made entirely of geometric shapes can be imbued with cuteness.

The Japanese have mastered cute (they call it *kawaii*) as well, from cartoon characters with huge eyes to miniature food. Japan enjoys a cute culture that is often a hair's breadth away from eerie; consider the "Sweet Lolita look" (think of the film *What Ever Happened to Baby Jane?*), where teens dress and parade around in the cutest girly gingham and frilly costumes as caricatures of fictional characters. Much of today's cute is in the form of Japanese exports, with Hello Kitty in first place.

Why is cute so popular? We just have a hunger—particularly for anything that makes us want to eat it all up.

Cutesy sketches for use in 1940s photo albums.

SEEING RABBITS

DISCOVER WHY THESE FUZZY LITTLE CREATURES PERSISTENTLY POP UP IN ART AND DESIGN.

On the first day of each month the promise of good fortune can be yours if you follow these instructions: At the exact moment of waking up to the brand new day, loudly say, "Rabbit rabbit rabbit."

A silly superstition? Perhaps. But what have you got to lose?

Not tempting fate is one reason why silly and serious *wabbits* (hares or bunnies) are as prodigious in art and design as they are in life. Think rabbit's foot. Paul Rand once said that a logo is like a rabbit's foot—"And you don't mess with rabbits' feet," he once admonished. But in art, the rabbit is not always a symbol of good fortune. Rabbits serve many functions.

There is the simple aesthetic pleasure of a beautifully rendered animal, as in Albrecht Durer's famous "Young Hare" (1502). There are the humane anthropomorphic representations that are accessible for children, as in Beatrix Potter's "Peter Rabbit" (1902). Rabbits are often cast in comedic roles, like Bugs Bunny, and are commercially manipulative, as in the Duracell Energizer Bunny. There are dozens of brand-name cottontails—the most famous are Br'er Rabbit, Jessica Rabbit, Roger Rabbit, the White Rabbit and the March Hare, to name a few. Speaking of brands, let's not forget either the Trix Rabbit or the Playboy Bunny (which started life as a stag because the magazine was going to be called *Stag Party)*. Then there's Harvey, Jimmy Stewart's six-foot-three-and-one-half-inch-tall invisible rabbit in the 1950 film of the same name. The metamorphosed rabbit-man and rabbit-lady have long histories in literature, theater, and art.

In many cultures the rabbit is a symbol of fertility. Can you guess why? It also appears in many myths as the trickster figure ("What's up doc?") who uses cunning (and speed) to outwit the world's dimwits. Which goes counter to the Hebrew *shfanim*, a term to indicate cowardice. In Korea and Japan rabbits live on the moon and make rice cakes; elsewhere they represent everything from youthfulness to godliness—the Great Rabbit, who gives life to the world. Christian symbology has rabbits both as signs of abundance and of vigilance, a reminder to flee from sin and temptation. Rabbits can be mean: The "killer rabbit" attack that involved a "swamp rabbit" that "attacked" President Jimmy Carter's fishing boat on April 20, 1979 and was beat away with the paddle. You can imagine how much fun the cartoonists had with that image.

Rabbits are indeed plentiful in graphic design—as logos and mascots—and illustration because there is an almost endless supply of imaginative possibilities. Rendering the rabbit is lots of fun, in part owing to its physical form—the ears especially—and the innate kinetic qualities it embodies. Rabbits can be cute, stylized, iconographic, impressionistic, expressionistic, surrealistic (jackalope), large, or small. Rabbits can be typographically made from an upside down R.

"Artist of the Year" painted sculpture
© 2007 Gary Taxali

The rabbit image dates back to antiquity (and earlier). An illuminated manuscript page located in the Municipal Library of Verdun shows an armored knight fighting an upright bunny while elsewhere in the manuscript bunnies can be seen in the marginalia playfully jousting with other animals.

The Easter Bunny is the king or queen of rabbit imagery. Originated by German Lutherans, the *Easter Hare* was originally the evaluator of whether children were good or disobedient, and it would dispense the appropriate rewards from its Easter basket. The egg-laying bunny came to the United States in the eighteenth century when German immigrants used the concept as a means to govern children's good behavior. Easter eggs represented fertility in general, but in certain rites, those that were colored red represented the blood of Christ. Brown (and now white) became the primary rabbit hue throughout the nineteenth and twentieth centuries when the image of the rabbit was refined and the chocolate bunny evolved into an archetype of everything rabbitical.

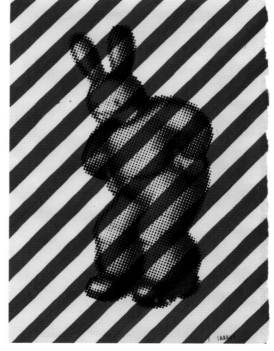

Rabbits are here to stay, their respective place in graphic symbolism assured. Or as Bugs Bunny so eloquently said: "Here I go with the timid little woodland creature bit again. It's shameful, but . . . ehhh, it's a living."

"Last Year's Winner," mixed media on paper © 2009 Gary Taxali

IN PRAISE OF THE ANTHROPOMORPHIC

MAN AS BEAST AND VICE VERSA IS THE TRICK THAT ILLUSTRATORS USE TO MAKE UNDER-THE-RADAR COMMENTARIES.

I've been asked by many students lately, "What is the future of illustration?" I usually refuse to answer on the grounds that I may incriminate myself by revealing an inability to be as wise or prescient as I am made out to be. After all it is hard enough predicting what's going to happen tomorrow, no less months or years down the road. But today I'm going to go out on a limb. I've decided that the next big thing is one of the oldest illustration conceits ever: anthropomorphism, "the attribution of uniquely human characteristics to nonhuman creatures and beings, natural and supernatural phenomena, material states and objects or abstract concepts."

On what do I base this pronouncement? Well, in hard times—and we can all agree the economy is not making life easy—people take refuge in fantasy and derive hope (or at least relief) from satire. These ingredients have historically resulted in anthropomorphic depiction in art and illustration.

But where does this tendency come from? Observe the platypus, whose prehistoric ancestor emerged from the ooze millions of years ago near what is now northern Australia, and is arguably an inspiration for anthropomorphic illustration. This aquatic mammal with beaver body and duckbill face may have been Mother Nature's attempt at satire, an early graphic commentary about the state of the primordial world. If this seems absurd, then consider the possibility that nature was playing with disparate forms, not unlike an illustrator sketching out an idea, never intending to end up with this design until becoming curiously smitten by the creature's strange physiognomy, then seeing in it a metaphor or symbol on which to build a global narrative. Is this too far-fetched?

Granted the theory has no scientific basis in fact (or even a toehold in that dubious pseudo-science), yet it is worth considering that animals have characteristics that are easily used to

illustrate human foibles, and some visionary at some time in history understood and exploited that. It can be proved, after all, that prehistoric man used animals as much for art as sustenance. Evidence of early interest in depicting animals pictorially can clearly be found on the walls of the earliest cave dwellings. Depictions in primitive cultures suggest that possibly the first attempt at interpretative, if not caricature, art integrated animals in transformative ways.

Although these primitives had no conceptual impetus to substitute man and animal, as the brain developed its powers of contemplation and imagination animals clearly came to embody and mirror certain human traits. It was, therefore, only a short leap from the artist accurately representing nature and animals found in the wild to transferring their familiar traits onto man. Art has long been a both a reflection and overt means of revealing of the human condition, so as man became more conscious of the inner self, animals would be used to express a range of characteristics, from the spiritual to the emotional.

The art of anthropomorphism is almost as old as image-making. The practice certainly dates back to early Egyptian slaves who poked visual jabs at their respective masters on scraps of papyrus or pieces of stone, veiling and protecting themselves by substituting kindred animal characteristics for human ones. The master never knew he was the butt of the joke, but the slaves understood. From then on, animals bore the symbolic weight of human folly. Whether employed for satire, comedy, or fantasy, animals (i.e., manimals) have long been effective metaphoric representations as criticism and commentary, because rather than target a single figure for ridicule, a particular animal carries the weight of all character types.

Somewhere along the sweep of history, anthropomorphism was practiced for the sheer joy of giving animals human characteristics—and vice versa. Few things trigger such visceral response as animals dressed in human garb. The incongruity of a beast acting civilized rarely fails to get a laugh. Lou Beach's sensual bunny (published in the *New York Times* science section) in a turn-of-the-century bathing suit, holding a lit cigarette, taking a rest from prodigiously promulgating her off-

spring, may or may not provide any viable human analogy, but it is a delight to ponder what the scene is all about. More comprehensible, but no less absurdly enjoyable, veteran cartoonist Ronald Searle's lion king is the perfect evocation of how the king of beasts might be if given the regal human trappings.

How did the lion become so regal? Who bestowed on it the king's mantel? Myths, fables, and all manner of imaginative stimuli have over centuries ascribed particular traits to beasts that have somehow achieved legitimacy, like the high stature of the lion, or the wisdom of the owl (which symbolizes learning), or the majesty of the eagle (which exudes power). Often the illustrator does not follow the familiar stereotypes. Sometimes it's enough just to make the animals fit into a personal metaphor—the elegant dog, the monarchial duck, the criminal dog. Sometimes culture has invested animals with meaning, yet most of the time the artist does this.

When the nineteenth century cartoonist J. J. Grandville depicted members of nineteenth century French society—merchants, politicians, and clergy—as various and sundry kinds of fowl, the reason was more often than not because the actual individual(s) he lampooned looked unmistakably like the animal in question. But when Ed Sorel filled a New York City subway car with a menagerie of types, it was because it is possible to look at everyone on the morning ride and mentally turn them into animals. No doubt on any given train, like Noah's storied ark, there are two (or more) of every animal type.

These are hardly beasts turned into humans or vice versa, but they derive from a history of turning the famous and infamous into other creatures that represent preceived or real characters and flaws. Alfred Le Petit (1841–1909) worked for the satiric journal *L'Eclipse* where in 1971 he created the bittersweet *Fleurs Fruits & Légumes du Jour*, a sampling is reproduced here.

CRACKING THE SMILEY

THE JOYFULLY SAD HISTORY OF THE UBIQUITOUS HAPPY FACE

The smiley or happy face is one of the most unambiguous symbols ever designed. What's not to understand about a bright yellow circle with two wide, oval eyes and a dimpled smile? It is goodness incarnate! Yet thanks to that itchy rash of recent emoji, like an infestation of bother some bugs, the innocence of the happy little guy has all but evaporated. With ubiquity comes scorn. With happy comes sad.

Now, Smiley is an obnoxious visual cliché as oppressive and overused as the phrase "have a good day." Heresy, you say? Goodness be damned! Its time to lay waste to a myth.

As Smiley's cosmology goes, Harvey Ball (1921–2001), an illustrator at an advertising agency in Worcester, Massachusetts, was commissioned in 1963 to design some public-relations lingo that would placate the employees of the State Mutual Life Assurance Company of America who were nervous about their futures because their company merged with another. Mr. Ball drew a smiling orb that he later refined into a universal symbol of goodwill. Yet smiley and frown face doodles had been used as signatures on personal letters, greeting cards and diaries before, and Mr. Ball might have been influenced by that.

He was paid forty-five dollars and never took out a copyright, but until he died in 2001, he held more than an emotional attachment. According to the Harvey Ball World Smile Foundation, Mr. Ball believed "that each one of us has the ability to make a positive difference in this world." Any effort to improve the world, "no matter how small, was worthwhile." Remarkably, like other inexplicably popular novelties, including the Pet Rock and Hula-Hoop, the smiley face triggered a nationwide fad in the early 1970s. An estimated fifty million smiley buttons alone had been sold, and the image appeared on countless other products as well, many of which are still licensed through Mr. Ball's foundation. In 1999 the USPS issued a smiley face stamp (I hope Mr. Zip was not hurt).

Harvey R. Ball is shown in 1998 with the smiley face he produced.

H. R. Ball, 79, Ad Executive Credited With Smiley Face

Mr. Ball looks somewhat sad, but his smiley graphic confection has had an infectuous impact on the world.

Another claimant for the originator of smiley had a plausible counter origin story. In 1989, Charlie Alzamora, then program director for the AM radio station WMCA in New York, told the *New York Times* that in 1962, a year before Mr. Ball's design, smiley was conceived as a promotion for the WMCA Good Guys disc jockeys. The distinctive yellow face was more crudely brush-drawn, with black dots for eyes and crooked smile without the dimples in Mr. Ball's rendition. So, there are two schools of thought about which came first. Whoever designed the prototype, however, would have to admit that the archetype goes back even further than 1962. Wikipedia shows a 1953 version used in an ad for the film *Lili* that looks like a replica of Mr. Ball's version, but smiley faces were simply not uncommon.

Another somewhat less direct source can be found in a 1962 issue of *Graphis* magazine titled *Le Soleil Dans L'Art* (The Sun in Art), a compendium of smiling and frowning suns. The inclusion on these suns of all facial features with emblematic rays might disprove this theory, but this extra detail does not entirely mitigate the true evolutionary relationship from sun to happy face.

The public got plenty sick of smiley in the 1970s, which fostered parodies including a happy face by Gahan Wilson with a Hitler mustache. But the public is fickle. Smiley is timeless and still used as shorthand for many things both serious and ironic. Like bunnies at Easter, it is a symbol for the ages.

HEY STINKY, YOU'RE TOO FAT, AND YOUR SKIN'S BAD TOO

HOW BIOLOGICAL MALADIES TRIGGERED A POSTWAR CONSUMER BOOM AND MADE AMERICA A BETTER PLACE TO LIVE

Body odor, foot rot, bad breath, dandruff, psoriasis, and even acne were not invented by American advertising. These normal biological maladies were around since humans emerged from the primordial ooze. Yet it was primordial ad men during the early twentieth century who made them into plagues of such biblical proportions only brand-name medicated pads, soothing creams, and scented sprays applied daily could possibly purge the demons from body *and* soul. B.O., halitosis, zits, flaking and peeling skin are nothing to sneeze at, but persuasive ad barrages made average Americans believe that possessing one or all was un-American and unchristian (cleanliness is next to godliness, after all). Madison Avenue's scourges were curable, but if they went untreated, heartbreak (i.e., "The Heartbreak of Psoriasis") was the ultimate punishment for all transgressions.

"Advertising helps to keep the masses dissatisfied with their mode of life, discontented with ugly things around them," reported an advertising trade journal in the late forties. "Satisfied customers are not as profitable as discontented ones." It was this dubious, though effective, incentive practiced during the post–World War II era (when the booming American economy was stimulated by the incredible surges of wartime production) that demanded increased consumption of sundries and medicinals to help prop up prosperity. There was no better way to herd consumers into stores than to elevate the importance of ersatz-hygienic values by instilling widespread insecurity through cautionary ads that attacked odor and smeared blemishes.

However, even this strategic paradigm, so endemic to postwar economics and aesthetics, was not new to postwar consumption. In 1919 an ad campaign for Odo-Ro-No, a deodorant for women, first invoked the initials "B.O." for body odor. Earlier ads for perfumed powders and salves merely claimed to be sweet smelling, but once the manufacturers of Odo-Ro-No launched their aggressive assault on perspiration and its odiferous gases, offering customers their patented "Armhole Odor Test," and warning that B.O. would hamper social acceptability, insecurity-marketing took off like wildfire. And it worked, especially with impressionable females who were the primary advertising targets, but with males too, who wanted to be attractive to impressionable females. As a 1950 ad for Lifebuoy soap showing one such insecure gent attested, "I'd always thought B.O. was something that happened to other people. Then I realized that B.O. was the reason I wasn't popular with others."

B.O. was one of the most damning scolds in American vernacular, and ridding the body of bacterially induced rancid vapors became a national pastime—nay, patriotic duty—opening the market for other brand name curatives. Listerine mouthwash, for instance, originally produced as a general antiseptic, was transformed by an advertising campaign that elevated basic bad breath from merely an unpleasant occurrence to a major blight. After World War I, when Listerine ads referred to bad breath as the pseudo-scientific-sounding halitosis, and promised "germ-killing action," the brand immediately captured a niche (that continues today) as the leading cure-all. The most memorable of these ads in the late forties featured the pathetic case of "Edna," who was "often a bridesmaid but never a bride," approaching her "tragic" thirtieth birthday unmarried because she suffered from halitosis—that "you, yourself, rarely know when you have it. And even your closest friends won't tell you."

"Quick-tempo socio-dramas in which readers were invited to identify with temporary victims in tragedies of social shame," wrote the late historian Roland Marchand in *Advertising the American Dream*, led to a new "school of advertising practice." Copy-heavy, poorly designed cautionary advertisements (resembling political manifestos) encouraged consumers to revile everything rotten smelling, from head to crotch to toe. A 1950 ad with a silly line

Bad breath and yellow teeth are no match for a flawless smile and fragrant persona.

ATHLETE'S FOOT
Fungi Feed on Steaming Feet!

● Did you know that Athlete's Foot fungi thrive on excessive perspiration and dead skin? That's why it's important to be careful when your feet perspire profusely. When the skin between your toes gets irritated and cracks open, Athlete's Foot is especially "catching."

CRACKS between your toes WARN YOU

Laboratory tests prove that Athlete's Foot fungi actually grow twice as fast when they feed on excess perspiration and dead skin. When cracks appear they get under the skin, through the cracks, and spread unseen beneath the tissues. Itchy, red toes and skin peeling off in whitish patches are signs you have dreaded Athlete's Foot.

Drench those cracks TONIGHT

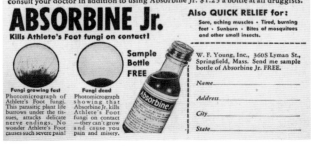

Play safe! Look carefully between your toes tonight. At the very first sign of a crack drench the entire foot with Absorbine Jr. *full strength,* night and morning.

1. Absorbine Jr. is a powerful fungicide. It kills the Athlete's Foot fungi on contact.
2. It dissolves the perspiration products on which Athlete's Foot fungi thrive.
3. It dries the skin between the toes.
4. Soothes and helps heal broken tissues.
5. Relieves itching, pain of Athlete's Foot.

Guard against reinfection. Boil socks 15 minutes. Disinfect shoes. In advanced cases consult your doctor in addition to using Absorbine Jr. $1.25 a bottle at all druggists.

ABSORBINE Jr.
Kills Athlete's Foot fungi on contact!

Fungi growing fast
Photomicrograph of Athlete's Foot fungi. This parasitic plant life burrows under the tissues, attacks delicate nerve endings. No wonder Athlete's Foot causes such severe pain!

Fungi dead
Photomicrograph showing that Absorbine Jr. kills Athlete's Foot fungi on contact —they can't grow and cause you pain and misery.

Also QUICK RELIEF for:
Sore, aching muscles · Tired, burning feet · Sunburn · Bites of mosquitoes and other small insects.

Sample Bottle FREE

W. F. Young, Inc., 360S Lyman St., Springfield, Mass. Send me sample bottle of Absorbine Jr. FREE.

Name_____
Address_____
City_____
State_____

---

drawing of a nondescript fellow underscored the damning point with the line, "Let's be frank. . . . Is your breath on the agreeable side? Don't run risks. Before every date use Listerine Antiseptic. It sweetens breath instantly."

Body odor and bad breath were, however, only two of the biological pariahs. "Personal hygiene became a crucial piece in the puzzle that upwardly mobile strivers were constantly trying to assemble," wrote Jackson Lears in *Fables of Abundance, A Cultural History of Advertising in America.* "Physical processes that had previously been taken for granted began to acquire ominous qualities, as one can see (or smell) in the changing attitude toward odor." Combining odor and dirt in ads tipped the consumer scales towards a national obsession with germ infestation. Lears cited an ad for Kleenex (the first sanitary disposable tissues) showing a nauseated housewife complaining that washing dirty handkerchiefs was the worst job on earth.

Yet even this aspect of the holy crusade for biological purity had its beginnings one-hundred years before the postwar consumer boom; as early as the 1850s, clean hands joined white skin, white bread, and white sugar as emblems of refinement and were cogs in the wheel of body management, a social construct that Lears refers to as "The Perfectionist Project." This enforced marriage of personal hygiene to regularity, and to efficiency on all strata of the social system underpinned most national consumer advertising.

Laxatives, for example, were promoted in the early 1900s to bring Americans in sync with the complex rhythms of modern life. As work hours conformed to Frederick Winslow Taylor's time/motion performance systems, daily

HE WASN'T THERE WITH "VACATION HAIR"

In his bathing suit, Harry ruled the roost with all the girls on the beach. But little did he reck with what the sun, sand and salt water were doing to his hair.

But away from the beach he looked terrible, thanks to "Vacation Hair." Water had washed away hair oils. Hair dried out, wild as the wind, impossible to comb.

That greasy stuff he used to correct his "Vacation Hair" didn't help. Observe how plastered-down and gooey it looked. What girl could yearn to caress such hair?

Then he tried Kreml. What a difference! Gone the dryness and stickiness. Kreml replaces lost oils without being greasy, refreshes hair, makes it easy to comb.

"VACATION HAIR" is almost impossible to avoid in summer. After swimming, golfing, tennis — after any exposure to sun, water, wind, dirt, recondition hair quickly, easily with Kreml. You'll be pleased with the results. For Kreml is not only a wonderful dressing, but a beneficial tonic, too — removes ugly dandruff scales and checks excessive falling hair.

Women too. Condition your hair and scalp with Kreml after outdoor exposure — and before your summer permanent.

SUMMER SHAMPOOS: Kreml Shampoo made from an 80% olive oil base is a splendid ally of Kreml Hair Tonic. It cleanses thoroughly, washes out easily and leaves hair easy to manage.

30

KREML

REMOVES DANDRUFF SCALES
CHECKS EXCESSIVE FALLING HAIR
NOT GREASY — MAKES THE HAIR BEHAVE

LIBERTY.

Any early series of Sterling Hayden still shows how dandruff can ruin a life, love, and more.

bodily functions were increasingly scrutinized with regard to the average workday. From this mantra of "regularity" another element of consumption emerged. Laxative advertisements assailed constipation as a greater menace to society than alcohol, so colonics were marketed to purge the innards of "intestinal toxicity." Kellogg's Corn Flakes was one such product born of the early individual health obsession: invented by Dr. John Harvey Kellogg, whose Battle Creek hospital and health spa (fictionalized in T. C. Boyle's *Road to Wellville*) was dedicated to purifying the inner temple of all toxins, and his toasted flakes were advertised like a modern medical miracle. While that particular approach was no longer effective by the postwar era, the "tastes good and is good for you" ethos remained fairly constant in advertisements designed to project a fundamentally unessential foodstuff as key to ideals of health and well-being that underscored American commercialism. This commercial ethos was rooted in so-called democratic freedoms, which consisted of "ignoring politics and worrying, instead, about the threat of scaly scalp, hairy legs, sluggish bowels, saggy breasts, receding gums, excess weight, and tired blood," wrote Marshall McLuhan in *Understanding Media*.

The Federal Trade Commission issued statutes in the late teens about "truth in advertising," yet advertising men sought ways to formulate new, harsher truths about real, but decidedly exaggerated maladies. "There's a womanly offense—greater than body odor or bad breath!" whispered the subhead in an ad for the feminine hygiene product called Zonite. Under the headline "How can he explain to his sensitive young wife?" a photo of somewhat disgusted young man with a comic thought balloon over his head read "There are some things a husband just can't mention to his wife!" Meanwhile Zonite was being promoted as the "modern miracle" because no other "douche is so powerful yet safe to tissues."

Outward appearances also loomed large in the minds of ad men. As early as the turn of the century, human fat was deemed a formidable enemy, yet oddly enough, although medical books warned against the dangers of obesity, many doctors claimed fat was an energy reserve. But when the advertising industry embraced the idea that being svelte was a marketable hook, "thinning down" became an American mission, and dieting a new religion. Which, in turn, raised the specter of an entirely new and continually replenishing market: American youth, a consumerist's dream. Even when ads were not aimed at physical restoratives and sundries designed to make "Lovelier Skin in 14 Days," pretty girls and handsome men in ads routinely had the same white, clean, perky looks. The demographic between ages fourteen and eighteen, known as the teenager, did not become a codified market until the postwar era (when both fashion and sundry marketers sold directly to it through magazines like *Seventeen*), but the cult of youth (twenty-five and under) had been celebrated by the advertising industry since the teens.

By the late 1940s young women had emerged as the quintessential American consumer for such products as toothpastes, deodorants, shampoos, facial lotions, soaps, and feminine products, as well as major appliances (cars were still the province of men, until the mid-fifties, when it was clear that women had a stake in the looks and performance of automobiles). Young women, particularly those who had sacrificed their luxuries during the war, were ready to be seduced by even the ugly, pedantic advertisements (which were published in abundance). They felt entitled to sharing in the new bounty, to be free from maladies, and look beautiful in the bargain. As for advertising, it asserted that civilization would abruptly end if these women did not actively contribute to the consumer boom that promised to make America a better place to live, love, and pursue happiness.

It happens to the nicest of Guys

ORDINARILY he was No. 1 on the hit parade as far as girls were concerned. But tonight he was getting the polite but cold shoulder over and over again. Something was wrong and he knew it...but he didn't know *what*.* It can happen to the nicest of guys.

The insidious thing about halitosis (unpleasant breath)* is that you, yourself, seldom realize when you have it. Moreover, it may be absent one day and present the next. And when it *is* present it stamps you as an objectionable person to be avoided.

Don't Take Chances

Why run this risk? Why offend others when Listerine Antiseptic is a delightful *extra-careful* precaution against unpleasant breath when not of systemic origin?

You simply rinse the mouth with Listerine Antiseptic and, lo!...your breath becomes fresher, cleaner, sweeter, less likely to offend...stays that way, too, for hours in most cases.

When you want to be at your best, never, never omit this *extra-careful* precaution against offending.

LAMBERT PHARMACAL CO., *St. Louis*, Mo.

Before any date
LISTERINE ANTISEPTIC
the extra-careful precaution

P.S. IT'S NEW! Have you tried Listerine TOOTH PASTE, the MINTY 3-way prescription for your teeth?

Modern medicine can do wonders for foot smells and breath odor.

GRAPHIC DESIGN AS CULTURAL MEMORY

GRAPHIC DESIGN AS CULTURAL MEMORY

—

THERE IS SOMETHING ABOUT GRAPHIC DESIGN THAT IS TIMELESS EVEN WHILE BEING TIMELY. THE CHRONOLOGICAL AGE OF DESIGNERS RARELY MATTERS BECAUSE CREATIVITY DOES NOT DISSIPATE OVER TIME—AT LEAST MOST OF THE TIME. IT IS IMPORTANT TO PAY HOMAGE TO SOME OF THE INDIVIDUAL DESIGNERS AND DESIGN PROJECTS THAT SHOULD ALWAYS BE REMEMBERED AND THE DESIGNERS WHO MUST NOT BE FORGOTTEN. HOW MEMORY IS RETAINED AND WHAT ONE LEARNS FROM REMEMBRANCE IS ESSENTIAL TO ALL. IT TAKES MNEMONICS TO RECALL THINGS AND FORCE OF WILL TO BUILD ON MEMORY.

LET THE EIGHTIES ROLL

THE OLDER YOU GET, THE BETTER YOU GET.

Recently I turned sixty, which is the new fifty. However, at fifty I often felt more like sixty, and now at sixty, I look a lot like forty but sometimes my body feels around eighty, which is the new seventy. Age is relative—aging is biological.

My own aging made me think more about even older graphic designers who have crossed into the eighties yet are as productive as ever. Unlike other arts, where genius usually presents at an early age, graphic design is like the proverbial fine wine: over time it achieves maturity—some of the time.

In 2011 a handful of celebrated designers and illustrators who were born in 1931 turned eighty. They joined a smaller group of flourishing octogenarians who are as vital, influential, and inspirational as they were back in their youth. Eighty may not be the new seventy, but if Seymour Chwast, Tom Geismar, Bob Gill, Peter Knapp, George Lois, Deborah Sussman, Tomi Ungerer, and Massimo Vignelli* (plus Ivan Chermayeff and Jan Van Toorn, born in 1932), Milton Glaser and Ed Sorel (each born in 1929) are any proof, eighty is just another calendar year in the continuum of fruitful professional and artistic design lives.

Talent doesn't come with an out-of-date stamp. Each of the "new eighty-year-olds" create art, illustration, typography, and design that rejects the stereotype of diminished capacity. If anything, their work is often more engaging, since long ago they went through the novelty stage of their careers. Free of the requisite need to be fashionable, they concentrate on design and illustration purity—and they are having fun. There is no mandatory retirement for graphic designers.

The question of aging, notes Jan Van Toorn, one of the Netherland's most critical design thinkers, practitioners, and educators, "brought to my mind the answer Dutch author and literary critic Jeanne Van Schaik-Willing [1895–1984] gave to the same questions in an interview at the age of eighty-five. . . . She talked about the successive and partly parallel or overlapping 'pla-

*Deborah Sussman and Massimo Vignelli both died in 2014.

teaus' she explored during her life—each time eager to examine a new field when she reached the horizon or edge of a former one. Looking at my own development, this metaphor was very insightful over the years. It made me understand how the 'findings' at the several plateaus—according to changing circumstances and acquired insights—keep you going, broaden and inspire your ideas and actions as a human being and professional."

How did this current batch of eighty-year-olds transcend time and fashion? Obsolescence is like quicksand; once a designer falls in it is extremely difficult to get free. So presumably equal parts talent, persistence, and ego increase the odds of professional survival.

Paul Rand, who was eighty-six when he died of cancer in 1996, worked energetically to the end. He literally designed a logo in his hospital bed. His latter work was arguably as relevant as it was in the 1950s when he typified American mid-century Modern graphic design. His three autobiographical monographs, published while in his late seventies and early eighties, codified his life's work but also had relevance for a younger generation. As a devout modernist he intuitively rejected design that was sentimental.

Not every designer can claim continued relevance, regardless of age. When Alex Steinweiss (1917–2011), the pioneer of American record cover design, turned fifty, he voluntarily opted out of graphic design, famously proclaiming that he was surrounded by "guys in fringed jackets" who wanted to choose their own designers. During the '60s rock era, Steinweiss's album covers, while beautiful, did not keep up with the demands of the zeitgeist. Only decades later, in his late seventies and eighties, was he resurrected as a historically important figure. Others, with less historical bona fides, became obsolete in a field that largely values fashionable approaches.

When I decided to write this article I immediately contacted Seymour Chwast, cofounder with Milton Glaser of Push Pin Studios and currently sole proprietor of same. We have worked together on many projects for more than two decades and he's always approached them with the same high-fructose energy as a kid playing sports. There is nothing eighty about him—seasoned maybe—but not old. Twenty years my senior, he's also my best friend. Yet his response to my idea was skeptical:

"What are you going to do for us? Get us more interesting work?"

Before I had a chance to respond, he added, "Who wants to hire someone who might die before the job is finished?"

He was joking. He is more or less in denial about this milestone, and it suits him. Chwast gets to his studio at 7 a.m. every weekday and draws, conceives, and draws more and more. On weekends he makes metal sculptures on satiric themes. He's done this for decades. The only thing that's changed over the years, and this is true for many others: he has trimmed down his staff and overhead considerably. Why carry a heavy weight, when it's much more fun to just do the work.

Other designers, however, more readily accept their new chronological designation. Deborah Sussman, known for creating the California post-Modern style through her firm Sussman Preja's design for the 1984 Summer Olympics, says, "It took me by surprise. I always thought I was exempt." Massimo Vignelli, who celebrated his eightieth birthday with the opening of an impressive gallery and archive space bearing his name—the Vignelli Center for Design Studies at the Rochester Institute of Technology (RIT)—says more fatalistically, "Without any doubt, it is a landmark. Mortality is becoming more familiar than ever, but at the same time is voided of fear. I have done whatever I wanted to do, more or less, and whenever I will have to go, I guess I am ready. . . ." And George Lois, who held the title of "Mad Ave's Wunderkind" well beyond the usual burn-out period in advertising, says that eighty "means that I'm getting closer to eighty-five, the age when I was always afraid I might have to stop playing basketball with all the young studs at the Y."

In our aging and ageist society, fifty had long been a line in the sand—a kind of beginning of the end—the tunnel at the end of the light. Not anymore. Owing to extended longevity and economic instability, retirement ages have been indefinitely postponed in many professions—today a work-till-you-drop ethic prevails.

Designers retire when they choose to, not when a corporation or government agency says they must. Barring catastrophic illness, talent is ongoing. If you've got it, you've got it forever. "I never thought of retiring," Vignelli admits, "therefore I thought that I will keep working until I die, if I am lucky. I may become unable, or clients will stop to come, in that case I will prefer to die."

Apparently, there is a fountain of youth. "Work has been the blood of my life," says Sussman, "but priorities are changing. I've become more distanced from micromanaging. I am thinking more." Lois echoes the work sentiment in his familiarly boisterous way: "I'd go out of my mind without having to solve a communication problem every day of my life. I'll die either at the computer designing with my son Luke, or on the basketball court with all my pals—with no regrets." He rattles off a long list of current projects including an ad campaign of Superfocus eyeglasses, an ad campaign for *Physician, Heal Thyself,* the branding and ad campaign for *Nail Your Mortgage,* a revolutionary process to nail down affordable, transparent mortgages in these tough economic times, "and a couple of others I can't talk about yet." And yes, he still plays hard-contact pick-up basketball games at least once a week.

Tom Geismar, who for fifty years has shared the marquee of Chermayeff & Geismar and has designed some of the most recognizable logos in America, says, "As long as you are able to work every day, and, importantly, enjoy it, why not keep doing it? My observation is that most people who stop working, and have nothing as demanding to replace it, rather quickly fall apart." Geismar is working on about five different projects, which he adds, "is about normal." Likewise, for Vignelli, being prodigious goes without saying; he's recently been working on several books, some packaging, some silverware, new re-edition of plasticware, the Vignelli workshops at RIT, and writing about design. What he calls "the usual."

Chwast's latest work is *The Odyssey* by Homer, "a graphic novel, written before I was born," he snickers. "Doing graphic novels has given me great satisfaction. Dante's *Divine Comedy* and Chaucer's *Canterbury Tales* were a lot of fun to do. My thirty-two-page picture books are tougher because every word and image are critical. I seem to make kids happy in spite of my indifference to their taste and needs."

I asked Bob Gill, cofounder in 1960 of Fletcher Forbes Gill (the forerunner of Pentagram), designer of films, musical events ("Beatlemania"), commercials and author of nineteen books, including the forthcoming omnibus *Bob Gill,* so far, if turning eighty has special significance. I should have anticipated that his answer, from the title of his book, would be "No!" Undeterred, I asked whether he ever imagined he would still be working this long. "I have no memory of ever thinking ahead professionally," he claims. "I went to Europe on a whim and stayed fifteen years. I returned to New York also on a whim, and I'm still designing, teaching, and thinking about books because there's nothing I'd rather do." Then he adds with a touch of pride, "and I still encourage my students to think independently, instead of regurgitating what the culture decrees to be 'trendy.'"

Tomi Ungerer, satirist, illustrator, children's book pioneer, and memoirist, who among other things altered the course of advertising illustration in New York in the '60s with his "Expect the Unexpected" campaigns, says, "With eighty you don't have much time left. And because I've trained myself all my life to have ideas, I am a slave now of too many ideas waiting in line, waiting to be used. I don't think ever in my life I've had that many projects on my shelves. I'm very grateful to have the energy to do them." Ungerer explains that his significant current pleasure "is the enjoyment to carry on with my thinking through collages and sculpture, and the missing volume in my autobiography of the New York years."

Van Toorn says he looks forward to this age for the space it allows him to "have enough time for the practical implications of a dialogic approach of visual production, bearing in mind the critical social, cultural, and linguistic worlds I became increasingly familiar with. From the start I made some space for this in my so-called 'laboratory work' or found commissioners interested in a contrary view on communication design. Later on, being a part-time educator there was more time to seriously invest in the combination of the language use and the liberating aspects of a politically oriented design."

Success obviously impacts longevity. The "new eighties" started their careers in a less competitive field. Their respective studios and firms emerged during a postwar economic boom, when corporate Modernism and cultural eclecticism were embraced as a means to further prosperity. Each of these designers made names for themselves in and out of the profession. "I feel that we in this age group were very fortunate to come into graphic design when we did," notes Geismar. "In many ways it was a new field, pioneered by those a generation ahead of us, like Rand, Lustig, Beall, Lionni, Schleger, Burtin, et cetera. It was a time when the culture was ripe for new ideas. The 1960s was surely a time of great upheaval, but also one of great opportunity. It was when our approach to design was set, and it certainly continues to influence my attitude to design."

Some of the "new eighties" retain the high profile clients they've had for decades; others have found newer, younger clients who value their past accomplishments, like Steve Jobs when in 1986 he hired in Rand to design the NeXT logo. Age has its privileges, when truly smart clients realize that the store of knowledge and experience is a huge benefit.

With age comes confidence—a stimulant by any other name. "Sounds like bullshit, but every job I do, I think is my best work yet. I wouldn't trade my career with anybody," says Lois.

"I never really thought in terms of 'a career,'" says Van Toorn. "Trained as a craftsman during the early fifties and at the same time interested in cultural, social, and political history, I had great difficulties to believe these worlds could ever meet. Later on I realized that our generation was very lucky to live in an era that gradually provided us with the desire to 'unlearn' and the critical answers and creative alternatives enabling us to break with the consensual thinking of the design industry."

When asked the inevitable question—what would they do differently if they could—Ungerer spoke for his peers: "This is a question one shouldn't ask. Since we are manipulated by destiny one follows what one has to do. It would be ungratefulness on my part to think I might have done anything else—I always learn from what I do, even if it was bad. I've been so spoiled by fate or destiny, as Edith Piaf sang, 'Non, Je ne regrette rien (I don't feel sorry about anything).'"

Vignelli shares Ungerer's sentiments: "My career went beyond my imagination. I am quite satisfied with the impact our work and theories had on the USA in the last fifty years. That is my legacy." Meanwhile Sussman muses, "life is really a series of moments which range from mountains to valleys and plateaus, via dreams, stairs, elevators, escalators, trails, air, and water, and friends and mentors."

However, when asked if Chwast's career went as planned, he paused for a moment and said, "No, I'm still waiting for the assignment that will be my breakthrough," but adds with a grin, "As Paul Newman said in *The Verdict*, 'This is the case. There is no other case.'"

"EVERY CHILD IS AN ARTIST. THE PROBLEM IS HOW TO REMAIN AN ARTIST ONCE WE GROW UP."

— PABLO PICASSO

PLAYBOY, THE LAST FRONTIER

NOW THAT NUDITY IS EVERYWHERE, IT'S NO LONGER IN THIS BAD BOY OF MAGAZINES.

When *Playboy* premiered in 1953 it attacked an ossified culture. It may not be politically correct today, but back then it enabled men to experience their sexuality free from prudish mores and preemptive censorship. It said sex was not unsavory or taboo. Hugh Hefner, who had briefly worked in the promotion department of *Esquire* (a tamer but no less controversial American men's magazine), invented a publication that would seismically alter the form and content of all magazines, and in the bargain incite something of a cultural revolution.

Hefner believed that men had the right to fantasize about being libidinous rogues who listened to cool jazz, drank dry martinis, drove imported sports cars, maintained hip bachelor pads. Through the magazine he contrived a culture that encouraged hedonistic and narcissistic behavior on the one hand and social and political awareness on the other. But Hef, as he is known, did not accomplish this alone. His message would not have been so broadly accepted if not for *Playboy's* innovative graphic approach developed by art director Arthur Paul, a former Chicago Bauhaus (Institute of Design) student. In the calculus of success much was riding on *Playboy's* premiere (Hefner invested his last dime and used his furniture as collateral to raise the initial eight thousand dollars); if it looked the least bit tawdry—like nudist magazines—the project would be doomed.

If Hefner had not enticed Paul to become the magazine's founding art director, it is possible that *Playboy* could have languished in a netherworld between pulp and porn. At the time that Hef was introduced to Paul, the magazine was titled *Stag Party* (after a 1930s book of ribald cartoons titled *Stag at Eve*) and the initial dummy (designed by cartoonist R. Miller) looked like a movie star/screen magazine with cheesecake photos and puerile cartoons (a few of them drawn by Hef himself).

"I was looking for a magazine that was as innovative in its illustration and design as it was in its concept," Hefner recalled in an interview. "We came out of a period where magazine illustration was inspired by Norman Rockwell and variations on realism and I was much more influenced by abstract art of the early 1950s and by Picasso. I was looking for something that combined less realistic and more innovative art with magazine illustration."

Art Paul studied with Moholy Nagy at the Institute of Design from 1946 to 1950. He was a serious designer/illustrator, and initially reluctant to join the fledgling magazine. He had a child on the way and needed security that he did not believe was possible with anything as speculative as this. But Hefner seduced him with promises.

The original inspiration for the magazine, says Hefner, came from *The New Yorker* of the 1920s and *Esquire* of the 1930s. Since Hefner was raised in a Midwestern Methodist home with puritan parents, "I believe that my life and the magazine were a response to that, and a direct reaction to the fact that after World War II, I expected the period to be a reprise of the roaring twenties. But it wasn't. It was a very politically and socially repressive time. Even the skirt lengths went down instead of up, which I saw as a sign. So the magazine was an attempt to recapture the fantasy of my adolescence."

Paul embraced Hefner's concept, but he was not pleased by the Stag title. "We made up a list of names that suggested the bachelor life," Hefner explained. "*Playboy* [originally the title of a twenties literary magazine] was in disuse at that point and reflected back on an earlier era, particularly back on the twenties—I liked that connection." Paul proceeded to develop a format that reconciled nude photography with the sophisticated fiction and nonfiction that became hallmarks of the *Playboy* formula. For Hefner, *Playboy* was a mission to influence the mores and lifestyle of men; for Paul it was a laboratory that turned into a model of contemporary magazine design and illustration.

Anticipating the first issue, "I took on the challenge in broad strokes," Paul recalled. "I said to myself 'this is a men's magazine; I want it to look masculine. I want it to be as strong as I can make it.' But I had tremendous limitations with the printing—the printers were doing us a favor by fitting us in. I was very limited in the number of typefaces and ended up using Stymie." The slab serif Egyptian was a perfect fit, being quirky yet bold. It worked well as a logo. For the interior of the magazine Paul employed white space to counterbalance the limited color availability of the first few issues.

The cover of the premier issue was critical. Only two colors were available. But conceptually, nothing could be more seductive than the photograph of Marilyn Monroe (a press photo of her in a parade waving to the crowd, which Paul silhouetted) next to the headline:

For this Hefner obtained for a couple of hundred dollars the centerfold photograph of Marilyn Monroe before she became a sex goddess from the John Baumgart calendar company. As for the absence of multiple colors on the cover Paul noted that it was a problem that turned into an asset: "I looked at magazines in a way I never had looked before. I found out how ours would be

FIRST TIME
in any magazine
FULL COLOR
the famous
MARILYN MONROE
NUDE

displayed, and I saw the other magazines it would have to compete with. Most used big heads and a lot of color and type. I felt that ours would have to be simple and so using the black-and-white photo with a little red on the logo was a plus, because it stood out no matter where it was displayed."

Paul initially wanted the logo on the cover to be small and in a variable rather than a fixed position, which meant he could move it around. Years later, however, it was locked in at the top. "Some of the more innovative covers happened in the early years," Paul admits, when he could freely use the logo as a conceptual element—and when he had more conceptual license to manipulate the models. Paul's *Playboy* covers were driven not by licentious half-nude women but by witty ideas and visual puns, which included its trademark bunny. Paul based all his cover concepts around different ways to inject the bunny into the design. Covers became games that

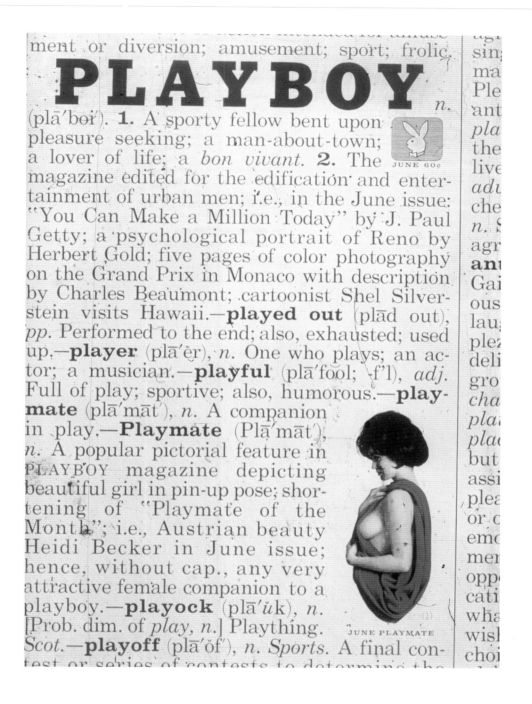

ment or diversion; amusement; sport; frolic.

PLAYBOY *n.*

(plā′boi). **1.** A sporty fellow bent upon pleasure seeking; a man-about-town; a lover of life; a *bon vivant.* **2.** The magazine edited for the edification and entertainment of urban men; *i.e.,* in the June issue: "You Can Make a Million Today" by J. Paul Getty; a psychological portrait of Reno by Herbert Gold; five pages of color photography on the Grand Prix in Monaco with description by Charles Beaumont; cartoonist Shel Silverstein visits Hawaii.—**played out** (plād out), *pp.* Performed to the end; also, exhausted; used up.—**player** (plā′ẽr), *n.* One who plays; an actor; a musician.—**playful** (plā′fool; -f′l), *adj.* Full of play; sportive; also, humorous.—**playmate** (plā′māt), *n.* A companion in play.—**Playmate** (Plā′māt), *n.* A popular pictorial feature in PLAYBOY magazine depicting beautiful girl in pin-up pose; shortening of "Playmate of the Month"; *i.e.,* Austrian beauty Heidi Becker in June issue; hence, without cap., any very attractive female companion to a playboy.—**playock** (plā′ŭk), *n.* [Prob. dim. of *play, n.*] Plaything. *Scot.*—**playoff** (plā′ôf), *n. Sports.* A final contest or series of contests to determine the

JUNE PLAYMATE

challenged the reader to find the trademark wherever it was hiding, whether it was placed on a tie clasp or fashioned from the legs and torso of a cover model.

Nobody could have predicted how world famous the *Playboy* rabbit would become. Hefner wanted a mascot from the outset: Paul's then-wife made a nascent bunny out of fabric for a cover. By the third issue Paul's original drawing of the bunny in profile is what became the "empire's logo."

Despite the predictable moral outrage in certain quarters, a large number of men (and an untold number of adolescent boys) flocked to the sign of the bunny. Yet Paul argues that while sex was a significant part of the entire package, it was not a sex magazine per se. He saw *Playboy* more as a lifestyle magazine, or as the subtitle said, "Entertainment for Men." Hefner wanted to present sex as a common occurrence, not a prurient taboo. By the end of the first year Hef began to take his own photographs. "The first centerfold was in [the] Dec 1954 issue, but it was early in following year when we got what I was looking for, a natural setting that looked less like a calendar and more moody." The important breakthrough came in shots of Janet Pilgrim, *Playboy*'s subscription manager, whom Hefner was dating at the time. In the picture Hef is in the background in a tuxedo with his back turned, while Pilgrim prepares herself at the vanity powdering her nose for a date. "I was trying to personalize it," says Hefner about the notion that nudity had to be connected to "art" or be considered obscene.

Paul's photographic contribution was to inject simple male-oriented objects, like a pipe or slippers in order to underscore a human element—or to give the girls "a smell," as the painter Richard Lindner once said about *Playboy*'s photography. But Paul was less interested in nudes than the other aspects of the magazine where he made his more a meaningful impact as an art director. This included feature page design and illustration.

His first love was illustration. Paul admired both Norman Rockwell and Michelangelo but admits a preference for the former, reasoning that "fine artists like Michelangelo were in dusty art history books, but the commercial illustrators like Norman Rockwell were on the shiny new covers of *The Saturday Evening Post*." As Paul became more professionally attuned, he was increasingly perturbed by the distinctions made by critics between fine and applied art, which reduced illustration to uninspired formulas. *Playboy* art was resolutely eclectic, drawing from surrealist, pop art, and post-pop schools. The fine art alumni included such known painters and sculptors as Salvador Dali, Larry Rivers, George Segal, Tom Wesselman, Ed Paschke, James Rosenquist, Roger Brown, Alfred Leslie, and Karl Wirsum. And Paul frequently published (and boosted the careers of) many top commercial illustrators, including Paul Davis, Brad Holland, Cliff Condak, Robert Weaver, Don Ivan Punchatz, and Tomi Ungerer.

Despite *Playboy*'s substantive contribution to art and design, it must nonetheless be credited with promoting negative female stereotypes, including false notions of beauty. Some have argued that Paul was complicit as art director. Yet such criticism must be balanced. For in the fifties and sixties sexuality was a new frontier—and bucking taboos was a political statement. Moreover, *Playboy*'s imitators, including *Rogue, Swank,* and *Cavalier,* offered unprecedented opportunities to designers and illustrators (some of them women) that were not available in other media. *Playboy*'s legacy is not just rabid (or rabbit) sexploitation; it was an entity that aggressively attacked a repressive culture while it settled into a new status quo.

THE NAME ON THE MASTHEAD

FRANK ZACHARY WAS A MAN OF MANY MAGAZINES—AN INSPIRATION AND MODEL OF THE EDITOR/ART DIRECTOR.

As a kid, *Holiday* was the magazine I loved most. It came into my house along with *Time, Life, National Geographic,* and *Boys' Life*, but *Holiday*'s beautiful photos, illustrations, and expansive size captured my interest. So did a name on its masthead under the words *Art Director*: Frank Zachary. I knew nothing about this romantic-sounding title, other than thinking it had something to do with discovering and publishing all the great artwork in the magazine. And, if my assumption were correct, then that's exactly what I would like to do after I graduated high school, if not before. That name on the masthead became my model.

Frank Zachary was born in 1914 and died in 2015 at home at 101 years old. He was one of the last of a generation of inveterate magazine impresarios, and his love for the medium was palpable.

I had the extraordinarily good fortune to meet Frank in the early 1970s, more than a decade after I had seen his name and long after he had left *Holiday* to become editor in chief of *Town & Country*. Others with whom he was close will doubtless offer professional and person tributes over the next few weeks—at least I hope so; mine is just a small piece of the enduring portrait of a monumental man who played such a role in my life that Veronique Vienne and I dedicated our book *The Education of an Art Director* to "Frank Zachary, art director, editor, patron of artists, designers, photographers, and art directors."

That was a heartfelt dedication but an insufficient epitaph. Truth is, there were very few real gentlemen and women in magazine publishing and Frank was undeniably rare. I have written before that he was the Catalyst-in-Chief, referring to the fact that neither as editor nor art director was his ego—and the power demanded from it—greater than the sum of his magazines' parts. As editor of the great, short-lived *Portfolio*, he basked in designer Alexey Brodovitch's splendid work. At *Holiday* and *Town & Country* he wanted others to accept their share of glory. His goal was to stir up the pot, find the new talents, and give them room to bloom and flower (excuse the mixed metaphors).

I first met him when a group of editorial illustrators and editors endeavored to make a visual satire magazine, somewhat like the 1896 German *Simplicissimus*. In addition to young, contemporary graphic satirists and commentators, the idea was to use some of the world's best: Tomi Ungerer, Ronald Searle, Andre Francois, Roland Topor, Edward Gorey, and others who were, in fact, part of Frank's stable of wonders.

A meeting was called at the home of John Locke, the fatherly agent for many of the European artists. In attendance were a few editor/writers, artists, and Frank, who was still actively running *Town & Country* (which was as far from satiric as one could get). But Frank always retained his equilibrium. His Hearst-published magazine may have been a showcase for debutants and squires, but he also longed to be part of something with bite—and offered ideas that were arguably more radical than some of the publishing neophytes in Locke's comfortable Upper East Side living room.

Despite the enthusiastic critical mass of participants, the nameless magazine never materialized, but I had met my "model," and we continued to meet a few times a year to discuss magazines in general. Invariably, every few months Frank would call to arrange a lunch. He called me! And what a wellspring of insight he was into the era of postwar American design that was so significantly documented in the three extant issues of *Portfolio*. Frank's varied life and history coincided with my interests: he worked for the 1939 New

From top: illustrations by Milton Glaser, Seymour Chwast, and—the best!

York World's Fair, published a line of photography books, commissioned Paul Rand to do some covers, was a good friend of E. McKnight Kauffer at a critical time in his life, and more.

After he reached ninety, Frank would call on the phone to ask how I was. It was me who should have been calling him. But he was a true gentleman to the end—truly interested in others with a mind that was catalytic. You know, even though his 101 years are over, he continues to be an inspiration, with no end in sight.

Illustrations by George Guisti

GO *WEST*, YOUNG ART DIRECTOR

MY HERO MIKE SALISBURY'S *WEST* OPENED MY EYES TO EDITORIAL PACING.

When veteran magazine art directors get together to drink mojitos and reminisce about the glory years before advertising pages broke up editorial wells and when covers were based on ideas not personalities, one title always gets mentioned: *West*. This storied weekly supplement of the *Los Angeles Times*, art-directed by Mike Salisbury, was a masterwork of design erudition, appreciated by those who could care less about design. It was typographically innovative in a pre-post-modern eclectic mélange of styles and forms, but that was the least of its attributes. Salisbury injected *West* with such an abundance of pop culture visual richness that it was more like a miniature museum than a weekly gazette. In the tradition of *Esquire, Playboy, Portfolio,* and *New York, West* was challenging and stimulating, the likes of which are rare in magazines today.

West covered a wide range of themes—mostly reflecting Salisbury's insatiable curiosities—from a feature on basketball that illustrates the tremendous size of centers and forwards by showing a life-size photograph of Wilt Chamberlin's Converse sneaker to a pictorial history of movie star pinups with a bevy of gorgeous silhouettes fanning on the page to an array of souped-up VW Beetles in all shapes and sizes. But it wasn't just his mind-tickling content. Salisbury's eye-catching layouts were three-dimensional, and like a pop-up book, the visual matter jumped up at the reader.

Because I was living in New York City, *West* was for me an imported delicacy, rare and savory. A few copies at a time came by mail, usually weeks after they first appeared. But timeliness didn't matter much. Printed on velvety newsprint, *West*'s saturated full-color images had a glowing patina. The illustrations and photographs were the crème de la crème of conceptual art, and consistently so. How many magazine covers and spreads are still recallable after thirty plus years? It is easy to remember one or two, but in *West*'s case, I really can conjure most of them: The "Goodbye, Ed Sullivan" (June 13, 1971) cover with a tear coming from the CBS eye; "Don't Swat! We're Your Friends" (August 29, 1971) cover with the actual-size flies against a plain background; and the cover with the bleached-out extreme close-up of Charlie Chaplin with only eyes, nose, mouth, and mustache staring off the page. Salisbury was also fond of parodying existing magazines, like the *Saturday Evening Post*, *Life* magazine*,* and *National Geographic.* Yet one of his cleverest covers was a photo of Von Dutch painting the *West* nameplate on a motorcycle gas tank.

Salisbury developed a what's what of great illustrative covers done by a who's who, including Milton Glaser, Edward Sorel, Robert Grossman, Charles E. White, John Van Hammersveld, Dave Willardson, Bob Zoell, and Richard Weigand. Salisbury also did his own illustrations and took photographs. His style was decidedly Southern, not Northern California. "San Francisco— the city in the North—is foggy, Irish/Italian Catholic and 'quasi-Victorian,'" explains Salisbury. "We know New York. New York is Rococo or Baroque. LA is streamline. To understand the differences between LA and New York contemporary illustration take a look at East Coast custom motorcycle-building—Orange County Choppers. They make bikes that purposely look like fire engines and the Statue of Liberty. Rococo or Baroque? I love what

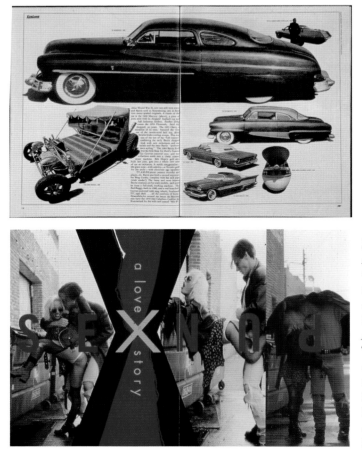

they do, but either classification you wanna give it, it is the Gypsy-wagon school of design. LA customizing is a belief in Futurism—a Jesse James West Coast Chopper is streamlined and cubist. The airbrush artists to go there were Bob Zoell and Peter Lloyd. The others were nostalgically mannerist except for Charlie White, whose complex compositions mixing scale and perspective defy categorization."

West was one year old when editor Jim Bellows, who created the original *New York* magazine in the early '60s for the *New York Herald Tribune* (and later developed *Entertainment Tonight*) was at the *Los Angeles Times*, and on the advice of Joel Siegel (later of ABC), asked Salisbury, who worked for Carson Roberts Advertising in LA (where Ed Ruscha and Terry Gilliam worked) to accept the job as art director. Bellows's assignment was to make *West* the vehicle for things California. *West* was originally like *Parade*. But this was the era when Otis Chandler remade the *LA Times* from a strictly San Marino Republican party newspaper into a world class publication. When

Mike Salisbury's *West* magazines were generation-defining publication designs. Many art directors would have given their most prized possession to be able to do what he did so well.

Salisbury took over art direction it was "all over the place, left-hand single page openers for editorial next to right-hand-page cheesy ads," he recalls. "I learned pacing and sophisticated typography at *Playboy* in my year there. And I learned the value of the editorial material—like Jann Wenner [Salisbury was also art director for *Rolling Stone*] selling déclassé rock and roll with classy writing. Hefner sold sex and lifestyle with solid writing, design, and production."

Salisbury was hands-on, but practiced what he calls laissez-faire and "the contributors were picked to give me their better thinking." He was also influenced by "the Bauhaus, Brodovitch, *Nova* magazine (David Hamilton AD), George Lois (for ideas), and Jean Paul Goude (for high concept), *The London Sunday Times Magazine* for inventing graphic information, Willy Fleckhaus of *Twen* (the best pacer ever), Lloyd Ziff, Dave Bhang (Lloyd is a real designer;

Dave introduced me to postwar art), Bob Grossman, Jim Bellows, Albert Einstein, and Issac Newton (a relative)."

Contemporary subjects were the mainstay, but Salisbury's special documentary themes, including the history of Mickey Mouse, Coca-Cola art (the first time it was published as "art," the visual history of Levis, Hollywood garden apartments, Raymond Chandler locations, and Kustom Kars were his favorite features. "A lot of these were my concepts and production. But design was not my sole objective, cinema-graphic information is a better definition," he notes. Of all the issues only the "Smack" cover, a skull with bright red lips, was controversial. "The same reaction people had to the [Barry Blitt] *New Yorker* cover about the O'Bama, I got for the 'Smack' cover, as in 'don't give me too much reality over Sunday breakfast.'"

After five years, in 1972, Otis Chandler killed *West* because it was unable to "generate enough advertising revenue to meet production costs," reported Dugald Stermer in *Communication Arts* magazine. Some magazines are better off dead, but *West* was a loss. "We died as readers, and we didn't even know we were sick," added Stermer, who proposed a means of resuscitating the corpse. "I have a belated suggestion for [Chandler] . . . that before they ax their baby (*our* baby), they mail their subscribers some variations of the following:

Dear Reader,

We're in trouble. *West* hasn't been attracting enough advertisers to make up the difference between production costs and what you pay to receive it. Since the magazine is really a partnership between you and the editors, we are asking you if you are willing to make up the difference yourselves. Our accountant has told us that if half of our 1,212,556 readers paid an addition of two and a half cents on their weekly subscriptions to the *Los Angeles Times*, that two and a half cents being used solely for the production of *West* itself, we could keep the thing going."

Of course, this never occurred (although was not a bad idea), and the magazine became a part of history. Salisbury moved to San Francisco to be art director of *Rolling Stone*, briefly injecting it with that *West*-ian panache, which is sadly missing from most magazines today.

BEING FORGOTTEN

ON EXISTENCE AND THE LACK THEREOF

Dying is easy, comedy is hard, they say, yet in the so-called *comédie humaine*, being forgotten is even harder on the psyche. Imagine being at the top of your design or illustration career one minute and entirely below the radar the next. The constant influx of great new design and illustration talent, and the ascent of younger art and creative directors, increases the likelihood of older practitioners being overlooked. Decades ago, I was a dismisser.

As a twenty-four-year-old art director of the *New York Times* OpEd page in 1974, I was the go-to person for illustration review and acquisition. I could help build a career by publishing a newcomer's work and revive a career, if temporarily, by reintroducing a veteran in the *Times'* pages. Both were exciting responsibilities. But there was another, less pleasurable, role.

Many illustrious designers and illustrators, owing to circumstance, had lost sinecures in their respective media outlets. Time may have taken its toll on their styles. Or their ideas were just no longer as sharp. Any number of reasons accounted for pedestals falling and careers breaking.

My own profound lack of experience and knowledge of history made me insecure, yet brash, which led to having little patience with the old-timers who came around. They had their chance; now it was my generation's turn. Only later, when I became a student of design and illustration history, did I realize how idiotic that was.

When I began at the *Times* many venerated illustrators like Andre Francois, Roland Topor, and Ronald Searle were represented by John Locke, an agent who made certain that snot-nosed art directors like me understood these artists' place in the pantheon. But there were many others of similar stature who were not so fortunate as to have such an advocate.

I recall one in particular, a Czech-born German cartoonist, Oscar Berger, to whom I owe an apology. Berger was a nuisance, I thought, routinely sending me work and stopping by without appointments to get work, which I didn't have to give him. I was dismissive, even rude. Little did I know until I began researching Weimar-era German satiric and comic magazines, that Berger

(1901–1977) was a prolific political cartoonist in Germany whose work appeared in many of the top magazines. He was one of the few artists allowed to cover Hitler's Munich Putsch trial in 1923 and was known for his theatrical caricatures. He left Berlin in 1933 when Hitler came to power, following the oft trodden émigré's path through Prague, Budapest, Geneva, and Paris before settling, in 1935, in London, where he contributed to *The Daily Telegraph, Lilliput, Courier*, and *News of the World*. He also produced posters and advertising for Shell, London Transport, and the Post Office. He was a roving visual journalist and was often drawing diplomats and world leaders at the United Nations. In the 1950s, he immigrated to New York, where he published a book on caricature, yet work was harder to come by and his reputation in Europe meant little here.

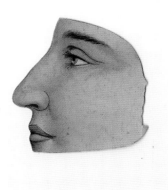

Berger was just the kind of person that right this minute I would want to spend a lot of time with listening to stories and capturing them on tape as oral history. He worked with many of those I considered masters, and he was considered at the time to be among that group. But other than a curt hello/goodbye I hardly exchanged words when I had the chance—and did not give him any work (although one of my colleagues would offer a spot now and then).

I often fantasized about meeting some of the heroic émigré masters, notably George Grosz, and asked myself whether I would give them work or not. Little did I know the answer was staring me in the face.

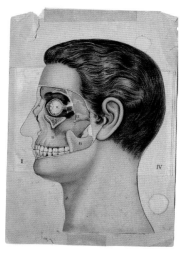

There were other displaced artists and designers who came through my doors on portfolio mornings, and some of them later turned out to be important enough to be written about in design histories. That they went on portfolio reviews was itself an indication of how easy it was to lose footing in this field.

A few years into my job, I knew the blinders had to come off. Not because I was becoming a writer of design and illustration history, but because it was the humane thing to do. I realized that a few decades later I could be Oscar.

One day your name and face is known. The next day you barely exist.

It's easy to fall on hard times and never recover. Conversely, take Alex Steinweiss, whom I helped to resurrect in the 1990s, and who did well enough in his life to enjoy his "forced" retirement. But there are other designers, illustrators, and photographers, as we learned in Adam Harrison Levy's touching *Design Observer* story on William Helburn, who did not fare so well in his later years. After having an incredible early career, falling into the void is much easier than simply dying—and that ain't no joke.

THE DEATH AND RESURRECTION OF THE GASTROTYPOGRAPHIC-ALASSEMBLAGE

THE RENOWNED, FOOD-THEMED "GREAT WALL OF CBS" HAS A NEW HOME AFTER TWENTY YEARS IN A BASEMENT.

When Laurence Tisch became CEO of CBS in 1986, he started cutting costs everywhere from the mailroom to the newsroom. Even the cafeteria wasn't safe. That's where the proverbial knife fell on a landmark typographic installation: the now-legendary "Gastrotypographicalassemblage"—the Great Wall of CBS—that had hung for more than twenty years.

At thirty-five feet wide by eight-and-a-half feet tall, this three-dimensional mural designed by CBS design director Lou Dorfsman and the typographic maestros Herb Lubalin and Tom Carnase took over one entire cafeteria wall of Eero Saarinen's Black Rock, the CBS Building on Sixth Avenue between 52nd and 53rd Streets. Dorfsman considered this massive frieze of custom-milled woodtype spelling out foods and food groups—from lamb chops to hasenpfeffer—his magnum opus, "his gift to the world."

That says a lot. Dorfsman was renowned for his graphic achievements, which gave CBS its corporate identity. He saw the value of integrating graphic with interior, on-air motion, and animation design. In addition to creating sets for Walter Cronkite's evening news show and the *CBS Morning News*, he oversaw every minute visual detail of the CBS head-

Detail of the newly
restored masterpiece.

The original wall with Louis Dorfsman standing proudly before it.

quarters building, selecting type for the numerals on the wall clocks, the elevator buttons, and even the elevator-inspection stickers.

Tisch, though, didn't seem that interested in typographic nuance or learning to say "Gastrotypographicalassemblage." The work was saved from corporate-mandated oblivion by the sculptural illustrator and 3D designer Nick Fasciano, who originally worked on the piece. Once in his possession, he stored it in his basement for twenty-three years as the ravages of time sent the piece into disrepair. Adhesives from the '60s that were used to secure the letters in place gave way, and many of the letters cracked off as soon as they were touched. The wall also contained sixty-five three-dimensional food objects that either deteriorated or were aged beyond repair. Eventually, it was acquired by The Center for Design Study in Atlanta, which in the 2000s began a fundraising campaign to support extensive restoration. "The wall is a window to the past that should be built up, not torn down," wrote preservation advocate Richard Anwyl in the *AIGA Voice*.

Shortly after Dorfsman's death in 2008, it was announced that The Culinary Institute of America in Hyde Park, New York, would fund the restoration and display it on their campus. Last week, after years of detailed renovation, the Gastrotypographicalassemblage was hung on ground floor of The Culinary Institute of America's newly constructed Marriott Pavilion and Conference Center. Rarely do works of typography earn such celebratory attention, but after what it's been through in the past few decades, some good news for the Gastrotypographicalassemblage is certainly overdue.

PAUL RAND, PAINTER

EVEN THE GREAT DESIGNER HAD A SECRET PASSION.

Paul Rand had more in common with Paul Klee than a four letter first and last name. For one thing, like Klee, he enjoyed playing with childlike hieroglyphs. For another, also like Klee, he used geometric forms combined with letters, numbers, and arrows that he transformed into sketches of animals and people. Okay, these similarities do not make twins (in fact, Rand had an identical twin who died when he was young). But there is more: Rand owned a couple of small Klee paintings (which were eventually sold to help pay for his archive at Yale) and, most importantly, his paintings were often like Klee's.

Yes, I said paintings. When thinking about Rand, most people don't consider him to be a painter or watercolorist, which indeed on occasion he was.

Here's a story. Once, on a visit to his comfortably modern home in eastern Connecticut, I said, "Paul, one of the things I like about you is that you don't pretend to be a painter." I had just previously visited the homes of two deceased graphic designers to gather some work for articles, and their respective children were pressuring me to write about their mediocre paintings. Not noticing the expression on Rand's face, I brazenly continued: "I mean, you do what you do so well, and you stick to it without having to prove you are also an 'artist.' I admire that, Paul."

Without a word, he took me by the arm, leading me into his bedroom where on three of the four walls were—gulp—paintings and watercolors. "Sorry," I said. "No offense intended." He smirked in that impish way of his, and we went back to the living room where the Klees, other Modern objects, and naïf artifacts were on display.

He broke the silence: "I am going to include a couple of those nonexistent paintings in a portfolio Mohawk Paper will publish." And then proceeded to tell me how he liked working in all media, including photography and painting and how it influences what he does and how rarely these "other things" are seen in print or elsewhere. Actually, he used excellent judgment insofar as the paintings and watercolors were appealing for their humor and craft, but they were paeans to Klee (and even Cezanne). They were not his true métier (pardon my French). They showed his interests and represented his eye, but painting was not his signature work.

Nonetheless, when the Mohawk portfolio was published, it was a veritable creative biography—and a real insight. Rand had selected eighteen disparate images, starting with a 1957 illustration of a paper-cutout hand with a striped top sitting on the finger. This was followed by Sweet Dreams, a 1970 photograph of his sleeping cat next to a pillow in wide striped fabric and this preceded Gate Sign, a 1975 photograph of a fragment of stenciled type . . . and so on. Each image was artfully selected, not to pedantically preface the next image, but in essence, to transcribe the visual dialogue he routinely had with all art forms—playful, deliberate, and serendipitous.

In this context the paintings made sense as studies or investigations of form. Yet on their own they still lacked—to my eyes— the verve and inspiration of his graphic design. Even the sketchy anthropomorphic cigar drawing he did for his longtime client El Producto had more distinction. And Rand obviously knew this or we would have seen more of his "personal" work in his books and exhibitions.

Recently, I was looking through the hundreds of outtakes from my book *Paul Rand*, to see if there was anything missing that should not have been cut. In fact, there were scores of great pieces from campaigns to posters, but nothing that truly irritated me by virtue of not appearing in the book. Then I stumbled upon a sleeve of transparencies of some of his paintings and watercolors, including a few sitting on a very serious easel (which I don't recall seeing in his home). They were presumably important enough to be photographed, but their respective whereabouts is unknown. Some were simple brush sketches, while others were more finished in a Klee-like manner. There is a prosaic feeling—a sleeping dog and vase of flowers. There is a quiet simplicity as well.

As a youngster, Rand was extremely adept drawing, coloring, highlighting, and otherwise doing what he called "Uncle Joe" renderings of real things. He gave that approach up pretty early in his career in favor of what might be termed abstract "representationalism." Eventually his drawing became little more than glyphs.

What is there to say about these paintings and watercolors? Are they building blocks or respites from the rigors of graphic design? When I said, "Paul, one of the things I like about you is that you don't pretend to be a painter," he had a knowing look. I don't think he wanted to be a painter, but he wanted to integrate art into graphic design, which he did so very well.

These paintings are not titlted, but they all have roots in the modern art that informed Rand's graphic design.

THE HAPPY FILM AS VOYEURISTIC PLEASURE

STEFAN SAGMEISTER SHOWS HOW A SLEW OF INTERPERSONAL MINEFIELDS IMPEDE HIM FROM ACHIEVING HIS OWN HAPPINESS.

Watching *The Happy Film*, the designer Stefan Sagmeister's semi-autobiographical feature documentary, will not make you significantly happier than you were when you entered the theater. But the fast-paced, painfully honest, stressfully contemplative movie, codirected with the late Hillman Curtis and produced by Ben Nabors, will doubtless trigger rushes of insight, empathy, and voyeuristic pleasure together with frustration, angst, and even annoyance, at times.

In the film, which premiered at the Tribeca Film Festival in April, Sagmeister sets out to analyze, define, and capture happiness as a concept, emotion, and commodity. But the esteemed graphic designer spends most of it showing how a slew of interpersonal minefields impede him from achieving his own happiness and impact his life, art, and design. Out of this discordance emerges a highly entertaining confessional that is equal parts reality show and experimental art piece.

The Happy Film actually began as part of a conceptual design project that includes "The Happy Show," a museum-exhibition-cum-carnival-midway. The spectacle has attracted over 350,000 visitors on its global tour. But while the exhibit encourages visitors to reflect on their own happiness, the film manages to be infinitely more personal.

The Happy Film is arguably a genre-defining work. Documentary filmmakers are often characters in their own films, but they're rarely this candid. Sagmeister's project captures his signature chutzpah, sure—but it hinges on an intensely personal search for why the root of happiness is so deceptive and elusive, revealing surprising insecurities about making lasting personal commitments other than his work, in the process.

A frame from one part of the title sequence that comes ten minutes or so into the film.

Sagmeister derives his happiness from upending the status quo in his work. For one of his more eccentric pieces, he used a razor blade to carve the details of one of his many design lectures into his naked chest and torso and used a photograph of the resulting scabs for a promotional poster. *The Happy Film* is like carving into his inner self. He is both investigator and the investigated. While the movie did set out to be autobiographical, as the production advanced, "I did not see a lot of things coming during the shooting," he told me after the premiere.

The Happy Film is not exactly the movie Sagmeister set out to make. While he had always intended the film to be somewhat introspective (or rather exhibitionist), he had not anticipated the pain that would befall him in the course of its production. "It started out as a design project with me in a rather fine mood," he told me after the premiere. "Then my Mum died. Our codirector died. Relationships fell apart." It sounds like a perfect storm of sorrow, but "I don't think it is ultimately a sad story," Sagmeister says. "It's about what a mess life really is." And all captured on film, to boot.

The Happy Film is divided into three sections. Each section follows Sagmeister for one month as he pursues happiness along one of three strategic paths: Meditation. Talk Therapy. Prescription Drug Therapy. The beautifully photographed meditation scenes are in large part set in Bali, where, after various failed attempts to reach nirvana, Sagmeister meets a former student with whom he falls in love. Happiness at last. But the relationship quickly deteriorates and sadness sets in. The therapy section records him in sessions with his psychotherapist who questions his ability to commit to others, despite an eleven-year relationship that just ended. This leads him to renew a relationship with a long-lost love back in Austria. When that relationship fails, depression ensues. In the drug section he engages a pharmacological therapist to monitor his intake of mood elevators. "I love pharma," he notes in the film. Yet ignoring the warnings not to make radical life changes as his meds are being stabilized, Sagmeister immediately falls for and becomes engaged to a woman who allows the rise and fall of the relationship to be documented on camera—these are the most emotionally taxing and uncomfortable scenes to watch.

Sagmeister has made a name for himself creating unexpected and uncomfortable designs, and he is fearless when it comes to letting the camera roll on himself and everyone else. "I had gotten and followed the advice from a very wise (and excellent) filmmaker to 'shoot everything and edit later,'" he says, recalling, among others, bedroom scenes that were left on the cutting room floor. What was essential to the story, and what would spill out, into oversharing, he says, "was on my mind a lot."

The Happy Film is not a motivational speaker's guide to wonders of happiness, and that's not what I wanted to see. Rather it is about one artist's search for bliss and the quagmires it caused. But there is resolution, so to speak. Sagmeister told me that for him happiness divides it into three parts:

"No. 1 Short-term Happiness, like a moment of bliss possibly lasting only seconds. No. 2 Mid-term Happiness, like well-being and satisfaction lasting hours or days. No. 3 Long-term Happiness, like finding what you are good for in life, which can last for years."

Throughout the filming Sagmeister maintained daily rating lists of his own happiness and it all comes down to this: "All periods of ten (out of ten) days had something to do with falling in love, all periods of one out of ten days were connected with a relationship ending. Falling in love in my case were connected to the No. 1 and No. 2 happinesses, work related to No. 2 and No. 3 type."

Makes sense to me.

Stefan Sagmeister stars as an artist in search of something called happiness
in an exciting, ambitious, and self deprecating montage of experiences.

IT'S EASY TO CRITICIZE ... NOT

WHILE MODERATING A PANEL, I LEARNED DESIGNERS WERE NARCISSISTIC AND SELF-CONGRATULATORY. SO WHAT'S NEW?

Convention was disrupted last Thursday night at Designism 2:0 when the sometimes "self-congratulatory" nature of the Art Director Club's social conscience–raising event was upended by *Vanity Fair* media critic Michael Wolf's unforgiving critique of design's do-goodery. The convention in question might be called "critical etiquette": When is it appropriate to publicly attack design and designers for work that is largely intended for social good? Usually acerbic commentary about design is left (often anonymously) to blog posts, while well-meaning public forums, such as Designism 2:0, are comparatively free of critical jabs and barbs out of respect for their socially redeemable intentions. Yet after observing presentations by educator Elizabeth Resnik about "The Graphic Imperative: International Posters for Peace, Social Justice & The Environment 1965–2005," ad person Jane Kestin on her Dove Campaign for Real Beauty, and designer Milton Glaser on his Darfur and new Iraq awareness initiatives, Wolf was asked (by me as moderator) to comment on the efficacy of the work.

He responded by branding everything as "banal," "trite," and "unoriginal." Then railed that design (and designers) were incapable of challenging issues or changing minds because their collective arsenal of alternative clichés, which has not changed in decades, is the same as mainstream ones that they sought to subvert. He further admonished the audience against doing anything if the result was not extraordinary. Instead, he said, just "read books, lots of books." The thud of two hundred plus jaws dropping was audible throughout the audience.

Known for a sharp tongue and strident critiques of media and media-makers, Wolf was relatively unknown to the design audience who came to Designism 2:0 to be, at least in part, inspired into action. Indeed this was an evening devoted to individual and collective activities that marshaled design to aid rural communities, voice political frustration, challenge common stereotypes, and attack the outcome of the current war. Rather than play along, however, Wolf sprayed buckshot, hitting various targets. He also voiced dismay that designers have not moved very far in their socio-political discourse. Yet with the notable exception of praising the '60s and '70s (the anti-Vietnam, pro-civil rights, and feminist eras) as the wellsprings of design acuity, he provided no alternatives, prompting one audience member to note: "It's easy to criticize!"

This statement had validity, given Wolf's wholesale indictment of designer pieties without an iota of what might be called "constructive criticism." But in fact, it is not easy to criticize at an event like Designism 2:0 and other such venues where designers gather to, well, feel good about their intentions and accomplishments or where, in this case, the goal was to motivate greater action in the public sector. Wolf had the temerity to ignore all virtuous motivations and brazenly attacked a few of the more iconic, if not heroic, results.

For Wolf it was *easy* to criticize—he had nothing to lose—he is not part of the design community. Yet it is doubtful anyone within the field (or in the audience that night) would have had the nerve to level such a public critique without issuing the requisite caveats and apologies for possibly stepping on colleagues' toes. Although Wolf opened the door for a few audience snipes at the Dove beauty initiative (including the main one, that the girls in the commercial were "not ugly enough" to really change deep-seated attitudes about self-esteem), the rebuttals were mostly impassioned defenses of design. Nonetheless, a number of post-event bloggers welcomed the opportunity to address the elephant in the room (how effective designers can be in the world of social concern) and were grateful for unfiltered criticism. Even Milton Glaser, who eloquently and convincingly addressed (rather than *defending*) his rationale for his long history of using design as a frame for communicating social concerns (he said he acts almost solely on a personal need to do so), agreed with the more pragmatic aspects of Wolf's analysis.

Wolf's provocative warnings about the danger of resting entirely on self-satisfaction if the end products are ordinary had resonance for some in the audience, while others clearly took umbrage. But the fact that he said it at all was, well, rejuvenating. The organizers may not have known at what level of intensity Wolf was going to engage these issues (and as moderator I was surprised by his initial barrage), but they understood it was necessary to trigger debate and knew that only an outsider, free from any intimacy with the design community, could accomplish the task.

The question raised by this is not whether design with social and political intent—or any design or advertising projects—should be critiqued and analyzed, but who at this stage is capable of raising such criticism free from seeming self-serving. Even "design critics" would not run too afoul of designers lest they lose access to them. Valid and needed criticism from within the field is often seen as tainted by overt prejudices, which often results in vituperative argument on blogs and elsewhere. So the most "constructive" aspect of this public critique was the fact that despite Wolf's acerbic, take-no-prisoners tone, issues were raised, myths were challenged, and, most important, civility reigned on the panel and throughout the audience. Criticism did not kill the discourse; instead it gave it new life.

INDEX

Italicized page references indicate an illustration.

ALLWORTH PRESS

BOOKS FROM ALLWORTH PRESS

Becoming a Design Entrepreneur
by Steven Heller and Lita Talarico (6 x 9, 208 pages, paperback, $19.99)

Business and Legal Forms for Graphic Designers, Fourth Edition
by Tad Crawford and Eva Doman Bruck (8 ½ x 11, 256 pages, paperback, $29.95)

Citizen Designer: Perspectives on Design Responsibility
edited by Steven Heller and Véronique Vienne (6 x 9, 272 pages, paperback, $19.95)

Design Disasters
by Steven Heller (6 x 9, 240 pages, paperback, $24.95)

Design Firms Open for Business
by Steven Heller and Lita Talarico (7 3/8 x 9 ¼, 256 pages, paperback, $24.95)

Design Literacy, Third Edition
by Steven Heller (6 x 9, 304 pages, paperback, $22.50)

The Education of a Graphic Designer, Third Edition
by Steven Heller (6 x 9, 380 pages, paperback, $19.99)

The Elements of Graphic Design, Second Edition
by Alex W. White (8 x 10, 224 pages, paperback, $29.95)

Graphic Design History
edited by Steven Heller and Georgette Ballance (6 ¼ x 10, 352 pages, paperback, $29.99)

Green Graphic Design
by Brian Dougherty with Celery Design Collaborative (6 x 9, 212 pages, paperback, $24.95)

How to Think Like a Great Graphic Designer
by Debbie Millman (6 x 9, 248 pages, paperback, $24.95)

POP: How Graphic Design Shapes Popular Culture
by Steven Heller (6 x 9, 288 pages, paperback, $24.95)

Starting Your Career as a Graphic Designer
by Michael Fleishman (6 x 9, 384 pages, paperback, $19.95)

Teaching Graphic Design
by Steven Heller (6 x 9, 288 pages, paperback, $19.95)

To see our complete catalog or to order online, please visit *www.allworth.com.*